The Artist's Roadmap

For Gregory David Scott
1988–2024

The Artist's Roadmap

Practical Strategies for a Career in Art

Delphian

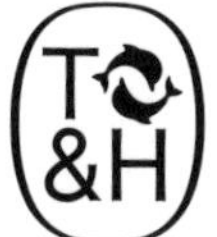

Contents

Foreword

When Benjamin Murphy and Nick Thompson asked me to contribute something to their first book, *Navigating the Art World: Professional Practice for the Early Career Artist*, I said yes immediately. We'd collaborated on a few projects at that stage, and I was already an admirer of their approach to curation and their support of emerging artists. I liked the cut of their jib. Benjamin and Nick have always been ready to say yes to any opportunity, no matter how crazy the deadline – a great quality that has rescued us from a scheduling dilemma more than once. They combined that responsiveness with an ability to deliver projects that intrigued and excited visitors. If their book was anything like their exhibitions then it was going to be unorthodox, experimental, bold, direct and dynamic. I think I may also have warned them that they'd be lucky to sell more than a few hundred copies of that book, and perhaps a few thousand if it took off. *Navigating the Art World* was published in the pandemic year of 2020 and the first printing was 500 copies. Benjamin and Nick knew their audience, recognized the need for the guidance given, and it has since sold more than 35,000 copies.

What you have in your hands now is a new book. It will be better than the last one because that is how Benjamin and Nick work. This guide may unlock opportunities at the start of your career or help you try new approaches if your career ambitions are not being realized. You need this book because becoming a successful artist, namely one who is able to live and work primarily as a practising artist, is a daunting proposition at present.

Part of the challenge concerns the word 'artist'. It risks becoming a redundant term devoid of meaning for a contemporary visual artist. An internet search for 'the most successful artist' yields results for popular musicians and performers. Look for fine artists and the results are the usual roll-call of long-dead historical figures that monopolize popular opinion about what art should and shouldn't be. Behind the scenes, tech companies are busy seeking to digitize and commodify creativity. At the other end of the spectrum, there is the pervasive conception that anyone can be an artist. The requirement to undertake extensive training, an apprenticeship or an extended process of development to earn the title of 'artist' has given way to a fast-track label that can be applied with the first fruits of self-expression. I can boil an egg, but that doesn't make me a chef. These trends mean you have to work harder to be noticed and recognized. There is a constant barrage of imagery being consumed daily, and fleetingly. How can you differentiate yourself, and how do you generate meaningful engagement with your work?

The insights in this book may give you an edge. I have assessed the advice for artists and art-world professionals against how we prospect for artists at Saatchi Gallery. The alignment of the guidance with how we go about our business is impressively high. Like all institutions and most commercial art galleries, we look for artists with imagination and talent. We often encounter these artists through our networks or prize submissions. But we also look for evidence of an artist effectively communicating with an audience or for the validation of peers. Furthermore, we look for artists with a proactive, collaborative and practical approach to projects. Within this book, you will find advice that helps improve your performance in all these respects, and it will help position you for those moments of opportunity that will hopefully come your way. Although this book provides a formula for potential success, it does not guarantee it. Most artists need luck, but it is possible to improve your chances of being lucky and to be more equipped to exploit the breaks when they happen.

Be ambitious. Be honest (especially with yourself). Be professional. Be original.

Good luck.

Paul Foster

Director, Saatchi Gallery, London

Introduction

What you hold in your hands is the follow-up to *Navigating the Art World: Professional Practice for the Early Career Artist*, a book in which we attempted to answer some of the most commonly asked questions about what it takes to become a successful and happy professional artist.

Since we launched Delphian back in 2018 we have spoken at numerous events and given lectures at more than twenty universities and educational institutions worldwide. Our first book is also sold in university bookshops and features on course reading lists in more places than we can count. This has made it clear to us that there is more to be said on the topic of professional practice for the early-career artist, and there is unfortunately not enough rigorous and informed teaching on the subject. This is for many reasons that we don't need to list here, but ultimately artist's professional practice is often incredibly hard to work into the curriculum of university courses. Because of this, it falls to people outside formal education to make this knowledge available.

After the success of our first book, we took a few years to sit back and digest the response to it. Initially, we had no intention of working on a second volume, but the sheer passion and excitement people had for the first volume was so deafening that we eventually had to relent. We read through the messages and feedback we received online (as well as conducting our own research through social media) to get a sense of what you wanted to see addressed. There were points in *Navigating the Art World* that we will touch upon again here, as well as a lot of new topics that we either didn't include in the first book or didn't examine to the extent that we are now able to.

Within this book, we have discussed a lot of the technical and strategic issues that go on 'behind the curtain' in the art world, and addressed some of the concerns, insecurities and challenges that artists may face on what is ultimately a fairly challenging career. A lot of these things are simply not talked about enough; this book is our humble attempt to remedy that.

We believe it important to point out that there is no one route to success. No two artists' careers are the same, so there is no single way that yours must be approached. What we are presenting here are just some things we have learned along the way that we trust will be of use. We hope that this book will help you in your pursuit of success, but it's important for us to acknowledge that we are not infallible. In reading this book it is incumbent upon you to take this advice on board, to digest it and, again, to decide what to accept and what to reject. We hope it helps.

Our Philosophy

People are often surprised to hear that Delphian Gallery is just a two-person team. Both of us met in 2012 when Nick was working for a small magazine that did a feature on one of Benjamin's first exhibitions. Soon after that, we curated a very small and very unprofessional exhibition together in Benjamin's live/work studio and started sharing works we liked on social media. We never thought too much about what we were doing and never planned to launch a gallery that would one day lead to the publication of this, our second book. We have never had any outside funding or investment, and do not take a regular salary from Delphian (we both work creatively alongside our Delphian output). In the years between that first show and now we have curated upwards of fifty exhibitions, as well as launching a podcast, residency and annual open call.

We tend to go with the flow, fitting Delphian projects in among our other interests and responsibilities, and this allows us the freedom to take risks and keep things fresh. Many of the issues that lead to most galleries playing it safe aren't a concern for us, with no permanent space and no other staff besides the two of us. This means that we can pursue projects that excite us without worrying if they will make money or not, which is not something that most galleries are able to do. It also means that we can afford to host an annual free-to-enter open call exhibition and not take a percentage of the profits from works that sell.

People often ask why we aren't in a rush to 'scale the business' and the answer is always the same: working as we do is really the only way we can make it work. It allows us to keep what has become quite a significant part of our lives as a passion project rather than an all-encompassing business that feels like work. It is also precisely due to our small scale that we are able to use Delphian as a platform to support early-career artists that may not yet have found a home in more commercial-style galleries.

We love finding exciting artists and showing their work to the world, and Delphian is merely a platform with which we can make that happen. We have no plans to take over the world; rather, we are just two friends doing things that we think are interesting, exciting and worthwhile.

What Sets This Book Apart

Other books attempt to do what we are doing here, so why should you read this one over any other? It's a valid question and one that we can answer fairly succinctly: *you shouldn't.*

That's of course not to say that you shouldn't read this book, but rather, that this shouldn't be the *only* book that you read. At the end you will find a further reading section, which lists some other excellent books on this topic. Read them all, take notes from them, and use what you learn to build your own framework for how you go about the business side of your practice.

The Artist's Roadmap isn't our attempt to disregard any of what has been said before, and indeed we read many other books in search of knowledge when we were at the beginning of our art careers, too. Instead, we are trying to build upon some of the useful information that is already out there.

As you continue on your artistic journey it is important to always be learning, searching for new knowledge and using it to find your own way of doing things. This book is our attempt to add something new to that which already exists, and nothing more. Don't read this book *instead of* those others; read it *as well.*

The One Single Thing That Will Improve Your Arts Career

It's a bold phrase but we stand by it. The single best thing you can do to improve your arts career is this: *stop being competitive.* That's not to say that we think you should abandon the ambition and drive to progress that has got you to where you are today, merely that you should re-adjust how you measure that progress.

Competition is something we naturally use, not only to track our successes but also to spur us on and inspire us to continue striving for development. While it can seem like your career is comparable to that of any of your contemporaries, no two artists' careers are the same, and success is influenced by myriad different factors. Some of these may be visible, but many won't be. Drive and competition are not two sides of the same coin. It is possible to be driven without becoming competitive, and this abandonment of competition with others who are in the same boat will only make you happier.

Collaboration is perhaps one of the best things about being an artist. We are all facing the same struggles and insecurities, and if we were all to strive towards collaboration rather than competition, we would all be much happier and more successful as a result.

As artists, we should expect our careers to have both highs and lows. When we look at the careers of others, however, we are only ever seeing the highs. The effects of social media are varied, but one of the major downsides is that it can appear as if we are the only ones who aren't successful all of the time. Most people will only present their successes, and keep any struggles, disappointments and insecurities private. Social media presences are curated, and when using other careers as a benchmark to set expectations of how our own should be going, we can often forget this. To compare ourselves to any other artist is to compare the whole of our own career (including all its highs and lows) to only one side of theirs – the successful one. This is only going to make us feel inferior in comparison.

Secondly, there isn't a certain amount of success to go around. When one artist succeeds, we all succeed. If we consider sales, for example, when one artist sells well, this allows not only *them* to keep going, but the gallery too. Successful galleries can take more risks, and we may be the beneficiaries of that risk-taking ability in the future. When the art market grows and new collectors emerge, we all benefit from a larger pool of potential buyers. Therefore you shouldn't see someone else's sales as detracting from your own. There isn't a set number of opportunities that are being used up by your contemporaries.

That said, it's sometimes hard to see others get opportunities that we have been hoping for. While this can be disheartening, try to imagine yourself in their position and feel the same joy for their success as you would feel for your own. They are probably experiencing the same insecurities and worries about their career that you do; they just keep it to themselves in the same way we *all* do.

No artist truly feels secure, as we are all looking towards that next progression, trying to continue the growth and development of our careers. Even the most successful artists feel this way, as they not only have to sustain their success (which is hard in itself), but also be seen to continue developing without becoming stale or repetitive. With more eyes upon them, the pressure is even greater.

Comparing ourselves to others can be problematic in other ways, too. Seeing their success can encourage us to attempt to replicate it, and the way we instinctively do this is to try to reproduce their work and the way they make it visible. To emulate others' work is to make our own work less genuine, and in turn less original. This rarely succeeds and is often obvious to the viewer, which can actually *hinder* rather than increase our successes.

These artists may actually help you in unanticipated ways, too. As they are at a comparable level to you, they are likely to draw a lot of attention to your area of the art world as a result of their success, and so even if it is hard watching them pull ahead, realize this: by association, they pull you forward, too.

If you thrive on competition, as many of us do, then the most effective way to utilize this driving force is to turn it inward. Compete not with those who are in the same boat as you, but only with earlier versions of yourself. Strive to develop and learn beyond these former selves. If you do, you can only be going in the right direction.

Taking Care of Business

Most artists dream about being able to make a living from their passion. The romantic idea of working away in your studio without having to sell your soul to some other job that you don't care about sounds almost too good to be true, and unless you take things seriously, it may just be. An unfortunate downside of this ideal is that it neglects to recognize some of the less exciting, less romantic activities that it takes to succeed as an artist. We are talking, here, about admin.

Admin work cannot be neglected if you want to be a professional artist. Without it, success becomes almost impossible. It is easy to reject this work because 'it takes time away from my practice' or because 'I'm just not good at that kind of thing', but unfortunately it is probably just as important as your practice if you want to turn art-making into your career. No one likes tedious admin when the alternative is as exciting as creating art, but those who get it done have the highest chances of success.

As a professional artist, the list of tasks you need to keep on top of is very long. Aside from making your work, you will also need to: keep up with your social media; draft and update your CV and artist statement; update your website; file your taxes; apply for opportunities; write about your work; network with others; and undertake many other things that will ultimately lead to you having less time to create than you might imagine.

It's a worthwhile exchange, however. 'Art' work and admin work are equally important, and it's likely that your attention has been heavily imbalanced in favour of the enjoyable creative side for too long. Dealing with all of this admin will lead to *more* studio time in the long run, as once you have advanced your career to a certain point, you will be able to reduce the hours you work at your day job, or stop altogether. By neglecting these other responsibilities, you may be actively holding yourself back.

If there is a particular thing you know you aren't good at, then it is incumbent upon you to address it and work hard at improving, because no one else is going to do it for you. If you don't like using social media, for example, you need to find a way of getting it done, as it is currently by far the most powerful tool available to you. Ignoring responsibilities like this because you don't like them cannot be an option.

There are far too many incredibly talented artists who make spectacular works that will sadly never be seen. There are also far too many artists who make lazy and insincere work achieving great success. The former are likely not focusing on the admin and the networking, and the latter are probably excellent at it. Somewhere in the middle is where we should all aim to be.

If you take one piece of advice on board from this entire book let it be this: *make sure you are taking care of business.*

What Is an 'Emerging Artist'?

'Emerging' is a term used to signify where an artist is in the timeline of their career, and as you might expect, this is the beginning. Artists should expect to be labelled as emerging for a significant period of time, and this isn't something to try and escape from too soon. While it might seem derogatory, it really isn't. In fact, it's perhaps the most exciting of the three groups, the others being 'mid-career' and 'blue-chip'.

Emerging artists are often the most experimental, the most open to change and the ones whose work evolves and develops at the quickest rate. These artists often exhibit in smaller settings, either as a part of artist-curated projects or collectives, and the DIY aesthetic makes this type of collaborative happenings feel the most exciting. It is the stage in an artist's career at which gallerists and collectors love to 'discover' an artist, and this pursuit of discovery is something these people get great satisfaction from. What it doesn't mean, though, is 'young' artists, which is a term that is sometimes erroneously and damagingly used in place of the less exclusionary 'emerging', or 'early-career'.

'Mid-career' is used to refer to artists who have had a number of solo shows, and multiple works in museums or other major collections. These artists will have had a significant number of mentions in the press, and their shows will be reviewed by magazines and periodicals. They may start to have a secondary market for their work, as collectors will buy and then resell their works as their career progresses, are often officially represented by galleries in different countries and will be showing their works at art fairs.

The terms 'blue-chip' or 'established' are used once an artist's name is solidly cemented among the most significant artists of all time. They will not only be written about in arts publications but will also feature in more mainstream news and culture titles. Monographic books will be published that show a significant body of their work to date, and they will have retrospective exhibitions at large galleries or museums. The secondary market is where a lot of their works will be sold, and their galleries may have waiting lists of people who hope to acquire their work.

Despite how it may seem, none of these terms bears any relation to an artist's age, or to the quality of their work. An artist is likely to spend a very long time in each bracket, and the move from one to the next is rarely clear cut. Some feel the need to try to rush their way through these stages as a way to legitimize their careers or show that they have been actively working for a long time, but this is always fraught with potential issues. It is not the artist's place to decide when they are to be referred to as mid-career or blue-chip, and trying to place yourself in one of these brackets too soon will have only negative effects on how your career is viewed. It is important to have an understanding of what each of these terms means, but whatever term is used to describe an artist is usually something that the artist need not concern themselves with too much.

Is Art School Necessary?

The question should perhaps be 'Is art school an absolute necessity?' or 'Is it impossible to succeed if I didn't go to art school?' In a word, the answer to both is no. If you didn't or won't go to art school, you aren't as doomed to fail as you may sometimes be led to believe, so long as you are doing all you can to learn and develop on your own initiative.

There are many benefits to arts education, so it makes sense to list those first. Engagement in honest critique, in-depth research, writing and socializing with one's contemporaries can be invaluable in the development of your work and career. Constant reflection on your own work can help you be rigorous in advancing both your practice and your professional development. Honest critique from one's peers is incredibly useful and should be sought out whenever possible. Once you leave art school, this seems to dry up almost entirely. So a formal setting in which critique is a part of the furniture is an invaluable resource. One of the reasons the work of early-career artists is so exciting is that art students are wildly experimental in response to the new ideas they are exposed to, and the critique they receive.

Art school is also beneficial because it forces you together with a lot of other artists who are all at the same stage of their careers. Some of these will make similar works to you, and others won't. This heterogeneous melting pot encourages debate and the cross-pollination of many different references and sources of inspiration. Peer-to-peer learning is incredibly valuable, and is much less likely to occur outside a formal learning environment.

The networks that are made at art school sometimes forge life-long connections. Some artists continue to collaborate with others they met at art school, and the more people you know, the more opportunities that may open up for you later in life. Someone you study with in your twenties might be the director of a prestigious gallery in your forties, and you never know when these networks will lead to something exciting, even many years later.

In addition, going to art school gives you access to amazing resources and facilities, which may be difficult to find outside formal arts education. It also gives you a few years of total freedom from the pressure of sales or funding that exhibiting as an artist might produce, and this total liberation can enliven your creativity. Art school also provides you with (or builds upon) a framework of conceptual thinking that you can utilize long after you have graduated.

The flipside to this is that art school is also unfortunately sometimes prohibitively expensive. It can be elitist, or hard to get into, especially if you haven't studied art before. Not everyone has the luxury of setting everything aside to go to university, and all these factors (plus many more) can lead to some people avoiding formal art education altogether. Luckily, we now have the internet.

Is it possible to succeed as an artist without art school? Yes, certainly. However, without art school, it becomes incumbent upon you alone to ensure that all this continued learning is still being had independently. *All* artists need to ensure they are doing all they can to push their work forward, and that can be more difficult without the constant need to justify your work to a group of critical, like-minded and engaged contemporaries. It is possible to become complacent and allow our work to stagnate if we aren't continually interrogating it, and art school is a place where you are required to do just that. If you don't study at art school, you must ensure that you read and analyse significant art history and art theory, learn to talk and write about your own work, and forge those networks that aren't ready-made and handed to you as they would be on your first day of an arts course. These concerns are often what set art school graduates apart from those artists who didn't study formally. Fortunately though, if you make the effort to continue learning yourself it is possible to achieve similarly high levels of competency in all of these areas.

Are all these things difficult? Perhaps. Will they take time away from actually making the work? Yes. But is it possible? Absolutely. It is also incredibly worth it.

If you didn't go to art school and are concerned that this is hampering you in some way, let us make it clear that as long as the work is good, no one really cares whether you have been to art school or not. Admittedly, some galleries and collectors might look to the artist's CV for more information about the trajectory of their career to date, and the presence of a good art school on that list can give further validation in some people's eyes. No gallery that exhibits emerging artists will pass up the opportunity to show exciting work purely because of a CV. That would be bad business, and galleries that make bad choices do not survive. A lot of the tools that we must develop to ensure that our work really *is* good are learned at art school, but that doesn't mean that they can *only* be learned there.

Not going to art school isn't going to harm your career. If you are able to not get complacent, to stay hungry and motivated in the face of disappointment and rejection, and to continue to evolve your work, you will do just fine.

Going Full-Time

Knowing when to quit your day job and focus on your practice full-time can be a difficult thing to get right. Many factors need to be considered, and the downsides to getting this timing wrong can be very damaging. We are often asked for our advice on how artists can make this transition from part-time to full-time, and our advice is almost always *don't rush into it.* If you are finding yourself with not enough hours in the day, and more sales and commissions than you have time to make, then it might be the right moment. If not, it might be best to put off abandoning your financial security until you absolutely have to.

Many early-career artists feel that achieving this 'full-time' status is what legitimizes their position as a 'proper' artist. Being able to survive completely from your art is a big milestone, and for some, it can be tempting to rush into this too soon. The comparison to your peers, insecurity about the legitimacy of your work and the desire for ultimate freedom are all big driving forces behind this decision being made. Sometimes removal of the safety net can indeed spur us on, but when we are talking about people's livelihoods and their ability to pay the rent, this decision should always be thought about as carefully as possible. Quitting your job to become a full-time artist can be incredibly exciting, but relying on your practice as your sole source of income can have its own downsides.

Firstly, surviving off your artwork alone can be a very difficult lifestyle to get accustomed to. Your regular and dependable salary will be a thing of the past and you must develop a hardy character both to weather the less successful months and to continue to save sensibly when things are going well. You must be effective at budgeting, and able to ensure that any quieter periods are accounted for ahead of time. This is stressful and can limit your feelings of financial security, especially as it is always unclear how long these inevitable low periods will last. (Not too long ago the Covid-19 pandemic would have been unthinkable, and while many artists were still able to work during the worst of it, many were left feeling even more insecure and unsafe than before.)

This rigid focus on your finances can also have damaging effects upon your work itself. With such strict budgeting, you may feel unable to experiment with new and exciting materials or find yourself cutting corners that make your work look less professional. Not having to rely on sales alone to pay the bills can help you avoid making only what you believe to be sellable. The pressure to make ends meet can lead to work that is safe and repetitive, which in the long run hampers your progress and leads to a decline in sales overall. Meanwhile, being less reliant on sales can help you to continue to make experimental, exciting work that continues to evolve and progress – work that, in the long run, is only a good thing for your career.

A distraction from your work can also be a big driver in the development of it. We can sometimes become blind to our artworks via over-exposure, and five days in the studio are often less effective than two or three. Being able to switch your mind off from whatever you are working on for a while can help you to come back to it with a fresh mindset, and to notice things that are hidden in plain sight.

The life of a professional artist can also be incredibly isolating, and working alone full-time in the studio can be detrimental to one's mental health. Regular interactions with others (especially when these are completely separate from your work) are important. It can be easy to forget this when your job is also your passion, but an unwavering focus on any one thing can be damaging. When your passion becomes your job, some of what attracted you to that particular pastime may be lost. Deadlines and the pressure of sales can introduce stress into something that was once the very thing you turned to when you were seeking relaxation. To use a familiar aphorism, the grass is always greener on the other side, and many full-time artists miss the freedom to experiment and explore their practice free from the constraints that the pressure of continued sales can create.

There are of course artists to whom much of the above does not apply. They are doing so well that having a more regular job on the side is an unwanted and damaging distraction from the work itself. For those individuals, transitioning into being a full-time artist becomes inevitable, and if that is you then congratulations are in order. For all others, our advice would always be to not rush into that decision until it cannot be avoided.

If going full-time *feels* like a risk, then there's a good chance that your gut is correct, and you shouldn't rush yourself before you are ready. Too much of anything too soon is a bad thing, and the unfair pressure put upon early-career artists to 'go full-time' can lead to feelings of inferiority, anxiety and stress – none of which will do your work any good.

If you are concerned that you must go full-time to be a 'proper' artist, then know this: many artists continue to have other employment in some fashion, even if they don't make that knowledge public. There may be some who try to suggest that only full-time artists matter, but that says more about their own insecurities than it does about you. All you need to become a 'proper artist' is passion, drive and self-belief. Those things you clearly have in abundance, or you wouldn't have decided to buy this book.

Do I Need a Studio?

This is a question that all artists must ask themselves at one point in time, but as with everything, there is no single correct answer. Having a dedicated working space that you can go to in the morning and leave in the evening has its benefits, but there are also some negatives that you should consider when attempting to answer this question.

The reasons for wanting a studio are numerous. Perhaps you need a separate space so that your home life and work life don't collide. Using oil paint in your living room could damage your furniture, for example, and the fumes might not be something you want to inhale as you eat dinner or feed your children. Conversely, working from home can be great for people who need to work in the small windows of time that they can fit around other responsibilities.

The first thing we should get out of the way, though, is legitimacy. Not having an external studio for whatever reason doesn't make you any less of an artist. Many hugely successful artists don't have studios because they simply don't need them. Some create small works that can be made just as easily on the kitchen table; some work from the garage, a spare room or even the sofa in front of the TV. The only thing that impacts whether you are an artist is whether you make work. If you are reading this book, then you are likely to qualify. No two artists are the same, and neither are their routines – creativity comes in many forms. We get the work done as and when we can, and there is no sense in sticking to a routine or way of working that doesn't suit us. Depictions of artists in film can suggest that they all work in a frenetic haze of inspiration, often late into the night, while shunning society and all human interaction. This stereotype is an exaggerated fiction and can lead to feelings of inferiority when one sees oneself as not conforming to this romanticized depiction of what an artist is or does.

If your only option is to make work on the kitchen table while the children are eating dinner, then embrace it and allow it to become part of your story rather than the cause of negative feelings or imposter syndrome. Do what works best for you and don't allow anything to make you feel the need to do otherwise.

In terms of benefits, if you have a workspace away from home, you will have less to distract you from your work. At home, everything is vying for your attention, and you may find it hard to focus when chores, comforts and the television are all trying to tear you away from your practice. Some artists who do have studios purposely avoid getting things like soft furnishings (or even chairs altogether) for their studios for this very reason.

Not having to worry about making a mess can also be incredibly freeing, as can the ability to scale your practice up. Having a space that is only for your art can work wonders for its development as you are free to take up as much room as you have available, and to leave it in a mess at the end of the day if necessary. Some materials are safer than others, so working from home may limit what is available to you. It is always important to consider safety when working with dangerous materials, but having a dedicated working space is a good way to ensure that any potential hazard isn't a danger when you (or others) are not in work mode.

Working from home can be isolating, and the inspirational effect of working surrounded by other artists (even if you only occasionally bump into them in the corridors) can be formative. Getting to know your studio neighbours can lead to interesting opportunities and collaborations too, and the potential for inspiration is rife in such a creative environment.

That being said, there are also many benefits to working from home. If you work from home, you can utilize otherwise wasted windows of time in between other tasks. If your washing machine has ten more minutes left, you might decide to use that time to trim some paper or to stretch a canvas. This isn't possible if you have to travel, and being able to work in short bursts like this is also a good way to avoid long, energy-draining sessions of intense work in a studio, especially if you are only able to use it for one or two days a week.

Secondly, it's no secret that studio rent is expensive, and this is the key point upon which most artists weigh their options when deciding whether to get an alternative space. This is especially the case for those artists who have children, pets or other dependants who require a certain amount of attention. The need to find childcare, for example (and the costs involved), may lead to feelings of wastefulness or inadequacy if you don't sell enough work to cover this. Ultimately, someone's decision on whether to buy our work is not something we have much control over, and so feeling as if you need to sell *more work* to justify the cost of a studio can lead people to make more *sellable* work. Trying to make work that you think will be more sellable can lead you to create safer (and so less interesting) work, which could actually make it *less* sellable in the future. All artists suffer periods of inactivity; you might be busy with other things or be suffering from a lack of inspiration, but if you're paying a lot of money for a studio it can produce feelings of guilt. Unfortunately, this is rarely good for productivity and can become a vicious cycle if left unchecked.

Studio kitchens and bathrooms are also almost always bad. Many artists eat poorly when in the studio for this reason, and this can have a negative impact on both your physical and mental health – which should always come first.

Luckily, if neither of these options sounds like the right one for you, there are some hybrid alternatives available too. Many artists choose to share a studio with others, and this has many of its own benefits not listed above. For example, you can still have a dedicated workspace without having to pay the entire rent yourself. These can also be highly collaborative and inspiring environments to work in, as your studio mates will see your work as it is in the process of being made and can offer critique and inspiration where necessary. Other people will often spot things that we don't ourselves, so having them look at the works in progress from time to time can be invaluable.

There are many ways of organizing a shared studio: it could be a studio in which anyone who contributes to the rent can come and work at any time, or one in which each of you has your own time slot to access the space. If the work you make isn't messy or large, then a shared studio can be a good way to have an external location to make work without the need for a large, and expensive, space. Desk space is often much cheaper, especially if it's a 'hot-desking' type of arrangement in which no one has their own specific desk and instead whoever is present on any one day takes whatever space is available. Drop-in studios or workshops are also a great way to be able to pay for space when you need it, and not pay for it when you don't. Print studios are the most common form of these, but ceramic studios, woodworking workshops and other specialist spaces are out there if you search for them.

However you decide to find (or make) a place in which to work, make sure it's one where you feel both comfortable and productive.

Finding Lost Inspiration

All artists suffer from periods of low inspiration from time to time, but even if you know this fact, it can be hard to stay motivated when the ideas just aren't flowing. Ultimately, inspiration is valuable *because* it is fleeting, so it's important to accept these periods where it is absent and to have faith that they won't last for ever. If you find yourself suffering a bout of 'artist's block', there are still ways to avoid allowing it to force you into a period of low productivity at the same time. It can be very disruptive and frustrating to have to prime the canvas or tidy the studio while your ideas are flowing freely, so it's always a good idea to try to get as much of this type of mindless work done when you aren't compelled to create. There is a lot of admin involved in being an artist, so next time you aren't feeling the impulse to make, try to use these periods to do something that is productive but doesn't require a spark of inspiration. Often, simply having enough to do will help you find your inspiration again.

Inspiration can come from anywhere, so it's crucial we expose ourselves to as many different art forms and absorb as much varied material as possible. Inspiration sometimes strikes from the most unexpected places, and so to expose yourself only to what seems immediately connected to your own work is to avoid something that might instigate an idea that transforms it. Fine art, philosophy and art theory are all very rich sources and have inspired countless masterpieces over the years. Inspiration can come from anywhere, though, so we shouldn't limit ourselves to only these when looking for ideas. There really is no sense in rejecting something because it may not be academic enough. When we think about what artistic research is, we often picture dusty books in a dark library. In fact, *any* experience has the power to create strong emotional responses, and there is no reason not to utilize them. If you find particular value in certain types of films, TV shows, sports, music, hobbies or video games, then mine those interests for inspiration for your work. Ignore any compulsion you may feel to look only towards the 'highbrow' and instead use whatever you find creates the strongest emotional response. It will be more genuine as a result, and perhaps even unique, because if everyone is only referencing the same philosophers in their work, it would be no surprise to find that all of their work is incredibly similar too.

It can be tempting to feel as if we need to be overly intellectual in discussing what inspired our work, and this can lead some people to massage the truth unnecessarily. This helps no one, and ultimately makes the art world feel even more exclusive and closed off. Instead, celebrate whatever it is that inspires you to make work and try to dig deeper down into *why* it is so inspiring to you.

Another experience that can be transformative – if we let it – is exposure to things that we *don't* like. Avoiding a particular exhibition/film/book because of the preconceived notion that you won't like it can restrict the scope of what possible inspiration is out there. If we only expose ourselves to things that we know we like, or that conform to ideas we hold ourselves, then we run the risk of having too narrow a focus for any real experimentation or evolution to be possible. At best you may find some new and exciting way of doing something, and at worst you will have realized another way of *not* doing something. Both of these are useful lessons, and can sometimes be the most valuable of all.

Approaching experiences with as open a mind as possible can allow us to be receptive to flashes of inspiration when they happen, and this can only be a good thing for the work.

The Futile Pursuit of Perfection

Creativity is an outlet, and a way to express thoughts and emotions that cannot be expressed verbally. This complete inability to perfectly express how we think or feel can be crippling when we expect too much of ourselves, and can be liberating when we redirect our thinking.

Artists are perfectionists, but at some point all creatives need to realize that the perfection they strive for is unattainable. The sooner you accept this fact the better. If we were to attempt to achieve perfection (in any creative endeavour), we would never complete a single work in our entire lives, instead changing and editing it for all eternity. It sounds dismissive, but acknowledging our own fallibility allows us to work free from the disappointment of unattainable perfection, while also allowing us to continue to strive for it.

This can be applied to many areas of our lives. We often wait and wait until we feel 'ready', but with each step towards that readiness, three more options open out before us. This is ultimately a way of talking ourselves out of doing certain things that scare us, because we will never feel *fully* prepared.

If you have reached a point where you think your work is perfect, or that it cannot be improved in some way, then you are lying to yourself. If you are unable to engage in honest self-critique and ask yourself if you are playing it safe, it isn't ever going to get any better. Something that all artists learn eventually is that things will never feel ready. Continually chasing that feeling can also lead to something being overworked, which in itself is an issue we should strive to avoid.

Once you free yourself from these distracting and unreachable goals you will feel much freer in your work, and that itself brings you one step closer to the perfection we must always chase but can never reach. Instead, stop talking yourself out of things in pursuit of an unrealistic ideal, and get to work.

The Importance of Critique

As an artist you should *always* strive to develop your work. You cannot sit back and allow it to become repetitive or stagnant, as nothing is less interesting than an artist who endlessly repeats the same idea. Sometimes, however, it is hard for us to see what is lacking in our own work. This is where others can help.

Honest and constructive feedback is the most valuable resource there is, so seek out people who are willing to give you this, and once you have found them, nurture those relationships. True critique is given altruistically and should be received as such, even if we disagree with what has been said. It is a term that is often misapplied, as feedback, criticism and critique are not truly interchangeable.

When giving critique, it is important to ensure that what we say is useful. 'The painting is good' or 'I like your drawing style' might be nice to hear, but they aren't necessarily helpful comments. Affirmations are the most common form of feedback, but the least tangibly useful. Objective praise is a little better, but still not true critique. Something like 'You have drawn the proportions well,' while a little more in-depth, is still largely useless. This kind of feedback is often given by those who fear hurting your feelings, or who don't understand the purpose of critique and how it is given.

The same goes for criticism, which is critique but without the constructive element. It is often derogatory or dismissive and often isn't given in the hope of helping the artist to develop. Criticizing something that an artist has no power to control, or without presenting a solution, serves no purpose other than frustrating the artist. Instead, focus only on things they have the power to affect. For example, if someone has made an oil painting, don't suggest that it would have been better as a watercolour – unless they have time to make one.

True critique is the holy grail. It is both subjective and objective, utilizing an understanding of the subjectivity of the viewer, the context of the work and what the artist is trying to do. This type of critique is the least common but by far the most useful, as the person giving this type of feedback is truly trying to help the recipient to develop their work. Giving this type of critique is one of the most beneficial things you can do for an artist, but it must be done honestly and openly, and in only the most compassionate of ways. When giving critique, try to think about what is going to help the artist most. Consider the type of feedback that you would find most useful and try to be the one to give it when it is your turn to do so.

Many artists can be quite sensitive when their work is compared to that of other artists. It's not a thing to be feared, but unfortunately many artists do. Artists can take comparisons like these as the suggestion that their work isn't unique, and if you have drawn that connection then it's likely they have noticed it before, too. This doesn't mean that these connections shouldn't be raised (and indeed there are many benefits to doing so), but do it delicately. Likewise, you should be careful not to use a critique session to ask open-ended questions about the work. Every question should serve a purpose, and the answer should be used as a jumping-off point for more in-depth discussion. People often use questions as a way to avoid giving true critique, as they can seem deeper than affirmations or objective feedback. However, you should remember you are trying to help the artist, so if you ask a question, you need to give something in return. It's also important that you are clear with your critique, and that you and the artist both understand what it is you are trying to say. There are a lot of art-specific terms that we can use to discuss an artwork, and these may be used slightly differently in the art world than they are elsewhere, so make sure you do some research on what these art-specific words might mean within the given context and use them correctly.

It is important to receive critique openly and unemotionally. Giving critique is a hard thing to do, and getting defensive when someone misunderstands your work, for example, will only make the person offering their thoughts feel hurt, insecure and possibly even a little angry. It will also make them less likely to offer up true critique in future and could encourage them towards criticism rather than critique. Remember, everyone who sees your work will interpret it slightly differently, and that's not only okay, but unavoidable. Try to open your mind to as many interpretations as possible because none of them undermines your intention, or what the work means for you.

When an artist expects the viewer to interpret the work exactly as they do, they are only setting themselves up for disappointment.

In teaching, there is a well-known feedback approach called Rose, Bud, Thorn (we have added Seed) that we can use to ensure that the critique we are giving is as useful as possible.

ROSE Is something that is particularly strong in the work. For example, 'The colour palette successfully reflects the overall emotional content of the work and sets the vibe well.' This type of feedback is nice to hear, it is useful, and it feels nice to be nice. It's not the *most* useful of the four, but it is far more useful than giving affirmations or objective praise.

BUD Details something in the work that has potential. It should be an attempt to help the artist identify something in the work that could be improved, but not something that is problematic, for that comes next. Receiving this type of feedback is far more useful than receiving the rose type, so try to seek out buds (and thorns) as much as you can.

THORN Highlights something that distracts attention, could be disruptive or problematic in the work or is prone to misinterpretation. This is an incredibly useful piece of feedback to receive when given well, but has the greatest potential to upset the artist when given badly.

SEED Provides some kind of resource for the artist to research. If the work makes another artist, artwork or art movement spring to mind then be sure to mention this to them. Even if this connection seems obvious to you, it might not have occurred to them. If it hasn't, then the more obvious it seems to you, the more useful it may be to the artist. Even if you see others give the same resource, don't shy away from mentioning it as well, as a multitude of people pointing to the same reference will lead the artist either to really lean into the connection or alter their work so as to avoid it. Give as many of these as you can, and don't limit yourself to just other artworks or artists, either: films, television shows, songs, plays, video games, podcasts, publications, books and almost anything else you can think of can be incredibly rich sources of inspiration, so always be very liberal when giving these references as the artist themself will decide which to research in depth and which not to.

Why Read Art History?

Exposing yourself to what has gone before can be immensely constructive both for your practice and in the wider experience of being an artist. While it can sometimes feel counterintuitive to look back in order to push forward, it is essential to know what has gone before if we intend to make something truly new. The tapestry of art history is as rich as it is vast, and whenever we are lacking in inspiration, this is the first place we should look. Many artists choose to keep a few books close to hand for moments like this, and a quick flip through the pages of a book or a short scroll online can leave us invigorated and excited to get back to work.

As mentioned in our section on critique, associations will often be drawn between your work and that of other artists. Most people hate it when their work is compared to another's, as they take this to be an accusation of plagiarism or unoriginality. In reality, though, nothing exists in a vacuum, so there will always be another artist that your work calls to mind, and it's often better to lean into these associations than to reject them. To remind someone of another artist is a compliment rather than an insult, regardless of how it was intended. Simply by association, you are doing something right. While no one should strive to be derivative, it would be unreasonable to expect that everything we make is *entirely* original.

In addition, having an understanding of the artists or artworks that your work might call to mind will allow you to understand your own work better. If you feel strongly that your output differs from that of another artist who is often mentioned to you, understanding them and their work will allow you to justify your position much better.

Researching artists, artworks or movements that you *aren't* particularly interested in will also throw up a lot of very inspiring ideas, so don't limit yourself to researching things you know you like. There is always something useful to be found if you look with an open mind. Remember, it's possible to be impressed by a seminal work of art while also not admiring it that much, and an artwork's potential to be powerful, poignant and awe-inspiring is not dependent upon our own personal tastes.

Shared passions are also a great way to build relationships with others, and discussions about art and artists are a hard thing to avoid in the art world. If it is clear that you haven't immersed yourself in art history, this could be taken as a sign that you don't know the difference between good art and bad art. It could be construed as a lack of interest in art in general and could raise questions about how passionate you truly are.

Contemporary art also needs to become something you immerse yourself in, so don't limit yourself to the past. Art history is just the bedrock on which your vast knowledge must be built if you too hope to become a part of that history one day. There are countless other benefits of a continued immersion in art history and theory, which should never stop. It is enriching and inspiring, and will help your practice in a myriad of ways.

The Trappings of Social Media

Due to its popularity and the ease with which we can view a lot of content quickly and from the comfort of our own homes, social media has become the space where we view the majority of the artwork we encounter. We can see many times more artworks in five minutes of scrolling than we would if we spent the entire day walking around galleries. Seeing an artwork on social media is not a replacement for experiencing the physical work, but it is now often the *primary* way it is discovered. We are seeing digital facsimiles: tiny images of how the work appears at a small scale. The word 'images' is key here, as what is being viewed is rarely the artwork itself, but a hyperreal representation of that artwork, presented small and shiny on a backlit lightbox that fits in the palm of the hand.

Social media is not the best way to see art (or even a particularly good one), but when we have a device in our pocket that can show us thousands of artworks at the press of a button, it would be remiss of us not to utilize it. What should be considered, though, is how this new way in which we discover art has affected the actual artwork we see.

It is now easier than ever to show your work to the world, and almost all artists are doing so in some way or another. Most use social media to present their work, and the feedback they receive through different forms of engagement can affect how they evaluate their own practice. If something performs particularly well on social media it would be hard not to take that as an affirmation of its overall quality, though to do so is to risk misinterpreting this feedback. When this engagement dictates what your work begins to look like, you are in tricky territory.

What effect is this having upon our appreciation of these works, and second, what effect in turn has this had on the art world in general? Firstly, backlit screens by their very nature alter that which we see upon them. When viewed on a screen, a painting is going to appear brighter, more saturated and more vibrant than it does when seen in real space. If we were to experience a painting first upon a screen and then in reality, the difference would be striking. The real painting is likely to be darker and less vibrant, though with much more detail, texture and sense of dimension than a screen could ever convey. The same also applies, of course, in reverse.

Artworks that are low in nuance, with flat, bold swathes of colour, reproduce especially well on a small screen, and so it is often those types of works that attract the most attention on online platforms. Because of this high engagement, algorithms show the work to ever-growing numbers of people, causing engagement to rise exponentially and creating the impression that this is the best type of work.

Auction performance, records of exhibitions, the artist's backstory, collections the artist's work appears in and awards received are just some of the other metrics by which success (or direction of career trajectory) can be judged. These, however, are of very little interest to the majority of the art-engaged public and so have less of an effect upon the reception of an artwork on social media than the aesthetics of individual works.

This success in turn drives (at least partially), what is seen to be successful in the wider art world. High engagement online naturally means that this work is most visible to curators and gallerists, and its creators are then more likely to become a part of the pool of artists from which they curate exhibitions. This then influences the tastes of the public, as the validation given by these institutions reinforces the implied consensus of quality that high social media engagement suggests.

At least *some* artists are, consciously or unconsciously, tailoring their works so as to attain the best response online. This is done regardless of whether that is the right thing for the work or not, and despite it (in some cases) causing a dilution of the work itself.

As artists, we need to be cognisant of the effects of focusing too much on the engagement we receive online. We must use social media as the tool that it is, and take full advantage of it without pinning all our hopes and dreams on our work's online performance. Social media is not the art world; it is merely a lens through which it is viewed.

Putting Your Best
Foot Forward

If you have read our first book you will know that we are big advocates of artists taking it easier on themselves, worrying less and relaxing a little. All artists have the same set of concerns, insecurities and vulnerabilities, and when artists act like these don't exist, they can give the impression to others that they are the only ones with such worries. This is damaging to people's mental health, and the sooner we all open up a little, the better it will be for everyone.

For that reason, we would always recommend artists opening up a bit more and discussing these issues with one other. Social media is great for this, and it's not necessary that you be quite as cold and professional on here as you may be on your website or CV. Showing a little of that vulnerability is usually a good thing: it humanizes you in the eyes of all watching, and anyone interested in your work is also going to be interested in you as a person.

That all being said, too much of a good thing can be damaging. Being *too* open online can harm your career, and can discourage people from working with you. Any success in the art world is the result of collaboration – it's impossible to succeed without it – and this is something we must get used to. It's possible that some collaborative arrangements won't work out how you hoped. It's still important to not let that frustration impact how you interact with others. You may have legitimate complaints to be made, but posting things online in the heat of the moment is rarely a good idea. It is unlikely to solve anything and can give the wrong impression. If something doesn't work out and you feel corrections are needed, you should exercise all options first before resorting to airing these grievances on social media. (It is a tool in your arsenal, though – and a very powerful one. Some artists use this to warn others away from a particularly toxic environment, and sometimes people need to not be allowed to get away with bad behaviour. This is just a cautionary note to encourage you to try all other options of diplomacy first).

Professionalism is always important, even when using social media. Being open about any vulnerabilities is good, because this helps other artists feel less alone, but these conversations should be had among friends rather than out in the open on social media. As an example: we all go through slow periods from time to time, and sales aren't always consistent. However, discussing this visibly on social media is only going to scare off potential collectors, as any purchase is an investment and people need to feel safe. While it's true that many people buy art purely because they like it, that transaction should never feel like a risk. If you are exhibiting less than you would like, try not to display this too openly and give galleries or curators the impression that no one else wants to work with you: it can paint you in a negative light and suggest that there are some underlying reasons why you aren't being invited to exhibit more.

Showing some of your personality and your personal life is a good thing, because if someone is interested in your artwork, they will also be interested in the person who made it. Only content that can help the viewer towards a better understanding of your work (and of you as a person) should be posted, though. At the same time, you want to create some mystery, so try not to overdo it when posting about things that don't relate to your work. Remember that an artist who sells their work is essentially a small business, and so needs only to share updates that support messages that help that business to grow. Much like our personal lives, we should be discerning when deciding how much of our work to share. You want to share enough that it seems like you have a thriving practice, but not so much that the mystery of it is ruined. Sharing too much might damage faith in the quality of your work or your dedication towards it, as it could appear as if your priorities lie elsewhere.

Using sub-standard materials is another way that artists may be sabotaging their own careers without realizing. If your work doesn't look like it will last, galleries and collectors are likely to want to avoid it. Low-quality materials are fine if you aren't planning to sell your work, but if you are hoping for someone to invest their hard-earned money in your creativity, these should be as high-quality as possible. Photographing your work badly can also show that you don't take any pride in it. Take the same care with how you photograph and present your work as you did with the work itself, because the vast majority of the people who see this work won't see it in the flesh: they will see your photo of it.

As artists, we can sometimes become our own worst enemies, and so we should always ensure that whatever we do is not only best for the work, but best for our own wellbeing too. If we want to make our passion become our livelihood, it is important to think about what information we are sharing with the world and what we aren't. There are many pressures that come with being a professional artist, and it's important that we acknowledge these if we wish to address them – and also because others will realize that they aren't alone. This type of conversation is best had among friends and contemporaries who can help to reassure each other when these pressures are felt; we shouldn't allow such conversations actively to harm our careers by making them too visible on social media.

Being Easy to Work With

Being easy to work with is almost the best thing you can do to ensure that people will want to collaborate with you again in the future. Word gets around, and if you are difficult to partner with, not only will those that have experienced you at your worst not want to work with you again, but neither will anyone else they have mentioned this to. We should all strive to be polite, pleasant and collaborative in all arrangements, regardless of whether the person or institution we are engaging with reciprocates that kindness.

Unfortunately, no one is perfect, and relationships can sour despite everyone's best efforts, but if our instinct is to try to get along with others in any capacity, it will only help us in the long run. This all seems quite obvious, but it is well known in the art world that success (especially early success) can lead people to develop over-inflated egos that damage their reputation. In an industry that can at times hype up or cut down artists based on what is and isn't popular, it is especially important that we don't allow any success (or lack thereof) to change our character. This approach should be the default when interacting with anyone, from unpaid interns to gallery directors, and from other artists to collectors and critics.

While we aren't advocating that anyone allows themself to be taken advantage of, the avoidance of a dispute or disagreement should be a priority if at all possible. In the same way that bad news travels fast, so does praise.

If you are a pleasure to work with, others will hear about this, too. All working relationships are essentially collaborations, and so a certain amount of compromise is likely to be necessary from both parties. If you aren't prepared to compromise, then it would be unfair to expect this from others. This is not just the case for when you are working with an established gallery or curator, but also for when you are collaborating with your contemporaries. Working towards a shared goal is a beautiful thing, and when something comes together as a result of the combined visions of multiple participants, the result is often much stronger than the sum of its parts.

As in any career, you are likely to encounter some people with different values to you. Relationships deteriorate and collaborative partnerships end, but it is always important to avoid burning bridges and to conduct yourself with calmness and respect even in the most trying circumstances. While you may never consider working with certain people again, you never know what influence these people may hold, and a negative word (regardless of how true it might be) said about you can be the tipping point at which a certain opportunity is given to someone else. Even worse than this, though, is burning bridges in public. It is never a good idea to air your grievances, however tempting it may be, as this will make you look unprofessional, regardless of how right you may be in the disagreement.

Some of the most successful artists and galleries we have worked with over our combined two decades in the art world have also been the easiest to collaborate with, and it is no surprise. They have staying power precisely because people enjoy working with them, and this pays dividends. If you are a pleasure to work with, and are accommodating and generous with your time, it is likely that this will encourage others to approach you in the same way.

Not Losing the Joy

There is nothing worse for an artist than the feeling of motivation ebbing away after another application didn't get accepted or a show didn't turn out as you'd hoped. Being a career creative is something that requires a lot of self-motivation, so how do we continue to push forward when the enthusiasm just isn't flowing? And how do we look after our mental health when we work in an industry that makes disappointments and rejections so commonplace?

Your mental health should always come first, because success is irrelevant if it comes at the expense of your health. Moreover, future successes are harder to attain if your heart just isn't in it any more.

While it is important to acknowledge that we aren't professionals with the requisite expertise to advise you on mental health specifically (see pp. 62–70 for guidance there), here are some more general lessons we've learned over the years that can help us go a little easier on ourselves.

Despite how it may sometimes appear, success rarely happens overnight. Realizing that success is a journey rather than a destination (as clichéd as that may be) is incredibly freeing. We are artists because we enjoy making work, so if you can retain your love of making, you will be a lot happier than many artists for whom it has become a job. If we reframe what we see as success and instead see joy as its measure, we will all feel much happier and, in turn, be more successful. It can be hard to see our contemporaries progressing faster than we perceive ourselves to be, but it's important to acknowledge that no two artists' careers are exactly the same and someone else's success doesn't make your own any less likely. If you are moving forward, you are going in the right direction.

It is inevitable that you will be turned down for an opportunity at some point in your career. When this happens, try to ask yourself if there is something that can be learned from the situation that can help you in the future. There are no true failures, only lessons, and so when something doesn't go the way we wanted it to, there is always value to be found in the experience somewhere. This value might not be immediately apparent, but have faith and keep searching for it. There have been times when we ourselves have faced disappointments or rejections in the past that (at the time) seemed like huge disasters, but a few years down the line the realization that the right thing happened for the right reasons always appears.

In the inevitable moments you find yourself disheartened or frustrated at the way your career is progressing, or losing the motivation to make work, there are always things you can do to continue pushing forwards. Firstly, if taking a little time off is possible and you feel like it might help, then do it. Sometimes coming back to something with a fresh pair of eyes can help you to see it differently and to discover what wasn't quite right the first time. Powering through these lapses in motivation almost always results in bad work anyway, so if it's possible to give your mind some space from it then do so. On the flipside of this, some of us need a little bit of pressure to be able to get our gears turning, and regular deadlines can be a useful way to do this. This can be achieved by either seeking them out or creating them yourself. Setting easily accomplishable goals is also a good way to motivate yourself to tackle the big ones too – the more tasks we can tick off on a to-do list, the more we are compelled to tackle the larger ones.

If you aren't motivated to create but still want to keep working, you can always use this time to prime canvases or tidy the studio. There is so much extra work that goes on behind the scenes and not all of it requires a spark of inspiration, so perhaps use this time to do some of the mindless tasks that don't demand too much concentration. If you can't think creatively right now, maybe use this time to add up some of your receipts or do a small amount of your accounting. It's better to use this time of low inspiration than to have to take time out of your art-making when it is flowing well, so utilize it when it occurs. The added benefit to this is that it can become so mind-numbingly boring that you will eventually be aching to get back to your creative work. When musicians are warming up, they play scales, ensuring that their muscle memory is as adept as their creative decision-making. If you find that your inspiration is lacking, perhaps use this time to go back to sketching, attend life-drawing classes or try to hone your skills in some other area.

When you aren't feeling able to work on what would usually constitute your 'work', perhaps take some time to experiment with something new. There is great power in playful experimentation, both for the development of your practice and for your own happiness, so if you are in need of a pick-me-up, this is always a good place to look. Sometimes a fresh perspective is reached by looking in another direction for a while. Either this new direction will be the thing you were looking for to begin with, or it will give you some other understanding about what was wrong in the work that demotivated you in the first place. Either way, this is a good tool to continue moving forward while not getting stuck on something that is zapping your energy.

Taking Care of Your Mental Health

LORI FITZGERALD

Lori Fitzgerald is a director of psychotherapy and mentoring with over twenty-five years' experience in supporting artists and creatives with their mental health. She is also a Jungian creative coach and a business mentor for those working in the creative fields. She runs the Therapy Den practice online and is an artist in her spare time.

The term 'mental health' refers to one's emotional, psychological and social wellbeing. Your own mental health encompasses various aspects of your life such as your thoughts, feelings, behaviour and ability to handle stress, and how you relate to others. It is a dynamic and fluid state that can (and will) fluctuate over time as it is influenced by biological, environmental and genetic factors. 'Good' mental health contributes to one's overall functioning, allowing you to cope with the challenges of life, form positive relationships, work productively and make informed decisions.

Mental health is not just the absence of mental disorders or illnesses but involves maintaining a balance that allows individuals to experience a range of emotions, navigate life's ups and downs and adapt to changes. It is a holistic concept that acknowledges the interconnectedness of mental, emotional and social wellbeing, as well as your physical health. Promoting good mental health involves fostering and practising coping skills, accessing social support and addressing factors (whether nature or nurture) that may contribute to mental health challenges. So as an artist, how do you plan to look after your mental health?

Let's start with the all-important basics. 'Self-care' is a foundational framework that is essential so that you can be the best version of your creative self. It is crucial to establish regular self-care routines such as getting adequate sleep, good nutrition and regular exercise. Your success as an artist will depend on many factors, but without understanding why and how you feel your best, It can be difficult to be creative.

Ways to activate your most creative self include engaging in activities that bring you joy, rhythm and calm. Activities such as walking, reading, stretching, listening to music, dancing, intimacy, good nourishing food and achieving realistic goals in your daily life are imperative to help maintain your optimum creative state so you can create your best work.

In order to maintain a healthy mental state as an artist, it is important to define and implement clear boundaries between work and personal life. Having boundaries means knowing what's okay and not okay for you to take on in terms of time, capacity and wellbeing. Understanding your boundaries will support you in avoiding the mental and physical health state known as burnout. Burnout is often misunderstood as 'feeling a bit tired' but is actually a serious state more akin to chronic anxiety or fatigue. Burnout has recently become understood as a medical state that requires long-term support, and it can take months or even years to fully recover from it. To avoid burnout, you must learn to say no to things when necessary so you can manage your workload and the stress that this can create. Just as you would place bubble wrap around your art before transporting it, you should treat your mental state with the same delicacy. Ensure you have breathing room before, during and after projects, setting realistic goals and acknowledging small successes along the way. You should also schedule regular breaks during creative sessions to prevent mental fatigue, and regularly step away from the workspace to refresh your mind and avoid burnout. Do all this now, and then reap the rewards for your mental health and your creative practice in general.

Next comes community and connection, because being an artist can be isolating at times. The solid commitment to one's own practice can see many of us 'locked in' with our current creative project for days, weeks, months or even years. To remain healthy and functioning, consider your social and human connection needs as well. It can help to foster supportive relationships with fellow artists or friends who understand the creative process and the pressures you may experience both internally and externally from your chosen career path. With this in mind, consider attending studio meet-ups or going for drinks or a meal with other creatives. Maybe consider seeking out professional networking opportunities that interest you so you are able to experience more from your collective artist community and hopefully meet more like-minded folks. Attend other people's shows and gallery openings but don't neglect your primary relationships (partner, children, close friends, wider family) as these may provide solid grounding in what can be a busy and demanding world. Essentially lean in a bit more where you can, with the intention to connect. In therapy we see all connection as being potentially important in what can be an isolating field of work and practice. Therefore it's important to nurture personal and professional connections alongside each other.

Have fun in your connections, but also give yourself permission to have meaningful boundaries and not invest too much time in situations or relationships with people who drain your mental energy or wellbeing. The art world has some large egos in it and your time is too precious to become enmeshed in situations that don't make you happy. There are definitely some situations where it's okay to use your active boundaries and say a firm 'no thanks' – but you do need to get out from time to time, so decide what connections work for you and then set about finding ways to make them.

As well as staying connected to your community and the world, staying inspired and connected to your own practice is vital for your mental health. If your creative practice starts to feel like a chore and the joy is being eroded from it, then the balance between your art and your mental (and emotional) health may begin to falter. Continued learning and growing as an artist is important and will assist you in maintaining a sense of purpose and accomplishment. Attending workshops, classes or conferences to stay inspired and connected with the art community is one important part of continued professional (and personal) development. Staying connected to yourself as an artist and your chosen field of work is also hugely important. It's important you remain deeply in love with your creative practice, but for that to happen you sometimes have to take a peek outside of your studio and comfort zone. We are always learning, and this is a positive boost for our brains, our nervous systems, our bodies and our creative souls. Don't stop learning, either formally or informally, and be a curious sponge every now and again in order to let some new stuff in.

Managing feedback and validation is a hard-learned aspect of working within a creative field, and it's key that we all learn the difference between constructive feedback and personal criticism. You create work that you are proud of and may wish to sell. But if you are seeking to make money from your craft, you may feel even more in the critical spotlight, and that's understandable. Not one single person has ever created better or more brilliantly or more successfully because of being shamed by another, so you should celebrate your achievements and acknowledge the value of your own work first and foremost. Do this realistically and with honest self-compassion and, when possible, do the same for others. Essentially put your boundaries in place.

To access further constructive feedback and validation, consider creating a small group of trusted honest creatives around you. These may be teachers or tutors, your peers, a mentor, your partner, close friends or studio colleagues. Ultimately, you have to learn to navigate the humble zone of hearing feedback, taking from it what you feel is helpful and relevant, learning from it, but not allowing yourself or your work (and your mental health) to be dependent on the opinions and words of another for validation. There is not one artist whose work is beloved by all. Not one. Better to be appreciated by a set of people who truly and honestly appreciate your work than to try to be held aloft by everyone. To be liked by all is to embrace mediocrity, and there is actually some thriving to be done if someone dislikes your work.

There is also some important learning here around managing perfectionism. You have to understand in your very core that art is a process, and it's okay for things not to be perfect. Create for yourself first and foremost. Stay true to your aesthetic and practice goals. Remember you are doing this for yourself, and even a commissioned piece of work stems from a buyer's need to own your style and not some filtered version of it. It's not about the final piece being perfect, it's about it being a true, original, creative representation of your work and style.

Perfectionism can be a particularly strong trait among folk who are neurodivergent, so if you are autistic, have ADHD/ADD or are dyslexic or dyspraxic, you may be more prone to binary thinking and processing (black and white, good or bad, perfect or pointless). Acknowledge this within yourself and know your susceptibilities towards perfectionism and its equally debilitating twin sister, procrastination. If you struggle with the latter, consider using processing techniques such as working in short bouts of about twenty to thirty minutes (often called 'the Pomodoro Technique') and take regular breaks. Acknowledge and celebrate your artistic accomplishments, regardless of their scale, and make time to reflect on personal growth and progress over time.

Being an artist can be a feast-or-famine endeavour. It's rare for money to flow with abundance, and many creatives may have second or third jobs to survive. Looking after yourself, your mental health and your creative practice means not shying away from financial management. Whether you are in receipt of benefits, are accessing a multiple-figure trust fund, have a grant or investor support, or utilize different income streams to support your art, it's essential to develop a financial plan to reduce the stress levels that can be related to income and expenses. This is good for your mental health. Money is not a poison to shy away from, nor are you in any way a failure if you don't have enough. It's what we need to survive, to be healthy, and it allows us the freedom to pursue our hopes, dreams and ambitions, creatively or otherwise, so establishing a stable financial foundation to support your artistic endeavours is important. Feeling secure enough in yourself that you have the mental and emotional space to be the creative you wish to be may mean being really honest about what you can afford and how you are living. You need a realistic budget that allows for rent or mortgage payments, food and bills, before you can factor in art supplies, studio space, materials and any of the other things necessary for your practice. Some of the documented lives of the most famous artists in history elicit a rose-tinted view within us of poverty, but poverty is no joke, and they achieved what they achieved creatively *in spite* of poverty rather than flourishing because of it. Creative flow means not also trying to work with a deep anxiety to maintain survival at the same time. Create that budget, ask for support if needed, and action whatever you can safely to ensure you don't have to live and create in a place of chronic anxiety regarding your literal survival.

Therapy and counselling are also sometimes necessary. Therapy has come a long way over recent years, and feeling supported in who we are as individuals is imperative. It could be argued that each and every one of us would benefit from therapy at some point in our lives.

If you are managing *any* mental and emotional challenges at all, consider accessing support. It can assist you in navigating a great deal of the emotional baggage that we all carry on our personal path, while also supporting you to build the resilience needed for your future, including your creative goals and ambitions, and managing those tricky creative blocks.

There are different therapeutic frameworks you can choose from, and there is also coaching and mentoring for more goal-focused support. Some therapies are accessed due to specific mental health conditions, but a great many therapists now operate from an integrative perspective, which means the therapy you are supported with may include a rich variety of approaches and skills, one example being art and creative therapies. You may feel that you are already doing this to some degree within your own creative practice, but please don't discount the powerful support a creative therapist may bring to the room, and their ability to support your mental health in addition to your own artistic practice may prove integral to your creative practice and life.

Your mental health is as individual to you as it is important, and it's essential to find strategies that work best for you. If mental health challenges persist, seeking professional help should be supported and warmly encouraged.

The more you look after yourself, implement boundaries, create space between and around your work, nourish yourself, maintain grounding connections and meet yourself with mindful care and compassion, the greater your ability to succeed in your creative field, and by extension in the rest of your life. Being an artist is hard work, but also gorgeous fun, and you need to acknowledge your needs, wants and capacity, and to seek out the best for yourself at every given opportunity. Hold your own space within your creative field, and for the bits of life you may struggle with, know that you can get support.

Our Most Requested Questions

There are many questions that we get asked repeatedly by artists, and so in this section, we've compiled a list of the most common and answered them as succinctly as possible.

DO GALLERIES REALLY TAKE 50 PER CENT OF THE PROFITS FROM SALES?

Most of them, yes. And the good ones certainly earn it. Determining which do and which don't earn their share is the tricky part, but when you find the right gallery that helps to drive your career and work forward - one that is willing to take risks and show your work - then this is worth that 50 per cent. A side note here, too: 50 per cent is the industry standard and they shouldn't take more, but it can also sometimes be a red flag when a gallery takes less.

HOW DO I KNOW IF AN OPPORTUNITY IS WORTHWHILE?

Do as much research as possible before saying yes to something. If possible, speak to others who have previously worked with those offering you this opportunity, or look at who they have worked with in the past and see if the associations made by having your name listed alongside these is going to be right for you. Be open-minded, but don't be afraid to trust your gut. At the beginning of your career, it is often good to say yes to as many opportunities as you can, because as well as gaining exposure, you are gaining experience. Further down the line, you may reach a point at which you need to start saying no to things, but try not to rush toward that prematurely.

SHOULD GALLERIES BE CHARGING ARTISTS TO EXHIBIT?

On the whole, no. It is true that sometimes it can be beneficial to hire a space to show your work, but that's not the same as paying for a *gallery* to show your work. If you do decide to rent a space, it is important not to expect too much from them besides the wall space. If a gallery is charging artists to exhibit, they will often show any artists who are willing to pay. This means that the quality is often inconsistent, and that alone does not encourage visitors, press or collectors. The gallery also has no real incentive to try to sell or promote your work, as they have already made their money from the hire fee. Galleries like this tend to over-promise and under-deliver, and so if you are looking for a gallery to really promote and sell your work, this might not be the best option. They are often referred to as 'vanity galleries', and working with such a gallery may actually cause more reputable galleries to avoid working with you in the future too. Similarly, if a magazine asks to include your work for a fee, they likely have too small a readership to be able to cover their costs through advertising revenue or sponsorship, and being included probably isn't worth the fee.

It should be said, though, that if you plan to do *all* the promotion and sales yourself, and only need some walls on which to hang the work, hiring a space can be a very useful thing indeed. Hire spaces and galleries are entirely different, but when a hire space tries to pretend it's a gallery, all people are doing is exploiting the sincere aspirations of artists. If you hire a space in which to show your work, it is usually best to avoid pay-to-play galleries (and all the poor curation associations that these come with) and opt for some kind of empty shop unit or other multi-purpose space. You should also expect to have to organize all the promotion, sales, networking and invigilation yourself, but gaining some experience of all these things can, of course, be invaluable in itself.

DO I NEED TO LIVE IN A MAJOR CITY
TO MAKE IT AS AN ARTIST?

That's much less essential these days than it once was. We are now more connected than ever, so as long as you are using the tools available (such as social media, mailing lists and the internet) to keep in contact with the art world from wherever you are, there isn't as much need to be in a major city as there may have been in the past. The extortionate rent and availability of studio space in these cities is why a lot of artists are moving to more rural locations at the moment, which in turn often leads to more artistic spaces following (as in Margate in the UK). Cities are real hotspots for arts and culture, though, so moving away has its downsides, too.

HOW DO YOU CHOOSE WHO YOU EXHIBIT?

We find a lot of artists through our open call. Unlike most open calls, we look *only* at the work, instead of combing through your website, CV, list of exhibitions and press coverage. We hope that this makes the selection process as unbiased as possible and opens it up to as many artists as are willing to enter. Ultimately, though, we only really look at the work when selecting artists for *any* show. As we are a small operation with very small overheads, we can take chances on very early-career artists, including some who have never shown before. This allows us to be flexible and responsive to the submissions without having to do loads of research, and we can go with our gut most of the time.

WHAT DO I DO IF I WORK IN TWO DIFFERENT ART FORMS THAT DON'T FIT TOGETHER?

This question is often asked by people who make what they see to be 'fine art' as well as some kind of 'applied art', such as graphic design or illustration (it should be pointed out that this isn't necessarily a contradiction, and none of these terms is derogatory). If your output really does vary on this level, consider using a pseudonym for one avenue of your creativity, or ensuring that wherever you display these two distinct art forms stays distinct. Having two websites or social media profiles can help with the separation if you deem it absolutely necessary.

IS IT POSSIBLE TO SUCCEED AS AN ARTIST WHO WORKS VERY SLOWLY?

In the hyper-connected, fast-paced world that we now live in, it can sometimes feel as if artists need to be constantly releasing work in order not to be entirely forgotten. While attention spans may now be shorter than ever, no one is going to forget you exist if you aren't producing (and showing) a new artwork every week. Similarly, not going overboard with the production of works can actually *help* to build excitement for when you do release new ones.

I DON'T HAVE A COMMUNITY OF CONTEMPORARIES; HOW DO I CONNECT WITH OTHERS?

For many reasons, artists can sometimes feel as if they are working in a vacuum. This can be disheartening, and lead to their motivation fading. Luckily, with the emergence of the internet and social media, networks do not need to be forged face to face any more. It is easier than ever to find networks of like-minded people and to interact with them from the comfort of your own home if necessary. There is no excuse not to.

DO I NEED A WEBSITE?

Yes, you do. While it may feel as if social media has made artists' websites redundant, this is not the case. It is important to have a website, as the function that this serves is different from your social media. The content is static, and the format allows for more text (such as your CV and artist statement) to be uploaded, as well as for download-able content. A professional and up-to-date website can really benefit all artists, and will be the place any interest-ed parties will go to find out more about you after they have spent some time scrolling through your social media. Make sure to include your email address and contact details in a very visible place so that any interested parties don't have to do any extra searching to find them.

WHICH IS BETTER, CONSISTENCY OR EXPERIMENTATION?

The oft-taught trope at art schools is 'find something that works, and stick to it'. While this may serve some artists quite well, overall it is continued evolution that we should all strive for. There is nothing less exciting than an artist who makes the same thing repeatedly, and they are likely bored of their own work for the same reason. If you want a long and exciting career, and you want others to feel that same excitement about your work that you do, then don't put out the same work endlessly, expecting different reactions each time. If you're worried that by experiment-ing you run the risk of producing something not identi-fiably your own, consider the output of David Bowie or the Beatles – artists who experimented wildly – and try to find a song by either that sounds as if it was released by someone else. Ultimately, every Beatles song sounds like a Beatles song, and every Bowie album sounds like a Bowie album.

How Do I Create My Own Signature Style?

Many early-career artists are concerned with the idea of a signature 'style' and whether their work is original enough. The title question for this chapter is something we get asked a lot, and our first bit of advice on this point is that a slight rewording of the question is needed. What's important is not *creating* your signature style, but *finding* it.

When you're first starting out, it's a good idea to experiment by copying the works of others, playing around with different materials and making as much work as possible. While it may sound counterintuitive, copying the work of others is a great way to allow yourself the freedom to create, without worrying about how good or bad your work will be. It's not going to be something you ever exhibit or are judged upon, and so this allows you to work without fear. This type of creation is important, but it is key to think of it as an exercise, rather than a process by which you create your own work. The same can be said for life drawing, automatic drawing practices and all other exercises that we use to develop our craft. Think of it like a musician playing scales or learning to play songs they like: it helps you to get better without the fear of having to create something original.

Next, it's important to test out materials – to be truly experimental in how you select and use them – in pursuit of finding some that really excite you. The more you test out, the more options you will have later. Experimentation is key, so use as many different mediums as possible and make art in as many forms as you'd like. Eventually, two things will happen. First, you'll find a medium and a subject matter that you are so excited by that you can't help but explore. If you haven't found those yet, all you need to do is to experiment more until you do. Second, you will naturally begin to do certain processes the same (or similar) as you have done them before. In other words, you'll develop habits. Both of these things are what create a uniform, identifiable style – but they do so naturally.

Your 'style' isn't really forged; it is discovered. It is something that happens naturally, as a result of repetitive actions and essentially, as strange as it sounds, mental laziness. Let's take drawing as an example. If you draw things repeatedly, eventually you slide into doing certain things the same way each time. Your instinctual choices about what colours to use or not use, which lines and forms to include and which to leave out, and what art to make and what not to all contribute to what becomes identifiably your own style.

Over time, your own style will emerge naturally, so spend your time not in seeking it out, but in developing the tools with which it can flourish once it does.

Approaching Galleries

The question of how to approach galleries is *by far* the one we get asked the most. Unfortunately, the art world often seems impenetrable (and at times elitist) to early-career artists hoping to get their start in the world of exhibitions. 'Why are galleries so unapproachable?' is a common question, and the answer to this is quite simple: by and large, the default is for the galleries to do the approaching, and not the other way around. Some galleries do accept submissions, but the majority do not.

The main reason for this is time. Most galleries are only able to put on around ten to twelve shows a year at an absolute maximum. If we allow for half of them to be solo shows and assume the rest to be group ones containing around five to fifteen artists, that is fewer than a hundred artists per year. While that may sound like a lot, many of those artists will be in multiple shows with said gallery, and so the number of individual artists exhibited per year will be far less. Each gallery usually represents a select group of artists, each of whom will need a solo show roughly every one to three years, in addition to being included in group shows and fairs. Suddenly what sounds like a large number gets very small indeed and doesn't allow for many new artists (despite how much the gallery may want to include them). Most gallerists are avid lovers of art and are on the constant lookout for new and exciting work. All of these factors can lead to them having an interest in far more artists than they can possibly exhibit in one calendar year, and they will be discovering more all the time. Their time is limited, and when they are already feeling incredibly constricted in how many artists they are able to show, there is often not much scope for accepting submissions on top of this.

This can be a hard thing to accept, as waiting around to be approached by a gallery in what can feel like an infinite sea of competition can make it seem like nothing will ever happen. Luckily there are things that you can do to make this possibility more likely.

Let's say a gallery you like *does* accept submissions. Before you do anything, you should look at the kind of artists they exhibit, ensuring that your work aligns with the gallerist's taste, and that you are at a similar stage in your career to the rest of their artists. It is incredibly important that you understand the gallery you are contacting, because not doing so is also a huge red flag. If you are pitching yourself to a gallery that has never shown work that you could imagine your own hanging beside, it is safe to assume that the partnership isn't going to be a good fit for either you or them. This doesn't mean that they don't like your work, just that it doesn't fit with the particular aesthetic or genre the gallery is presenting. Likewise, if a gallery only shows blue-chip artists and you have just graduated, there is no real use in submitting.

If you do decide to submit, it is important to follow the gallery's submission guidelines. These exist to make everyone's lives easier, and by following them to the letter you are showing the gallery that you would be professional and easy to work with from the outset. The tone you use and the language with which you convey it are also very important. Being an artist requires a lot of self-confidence, but it is important to not allow that self-confidence to come off as arrogance. Remember that whoever opens your email is a person, and should always be treated with compassion and respect – even if your approach is turned down.

In addition to this, your approach should be highly personalized and show that you have done your research on the gallery. There is no excuse for copy-and-paste emails to galleries, and they almost never lead to anything. These emails probably don't even get opened by the majority of recipients, and those that do read them will probably block or delete your messages in the future. It is incredibly important that you understand the gallery you are contacting, because not doing so is also a huge red flag.

There is also always the chance that an opportunity to work together will present itself in future, and any impression you make upon that person should be a good one. Submissions are rejected for a multitude of reasons, but it is never out of spite. Try not to take any rejection as a rebuff of you as a person, and instead try to accept that for whatever reason, a partnership wasn't the right fit at the time. Sometimes galleries keep an eye on an artist for a while before inviting them to participate in their programme – either because they don't have space in the schedule at the time, or because they feel that the artist needs a little more time to develop their practice.

No rejection is a rejection *in perpetuity* – and as time passes, views may change.

It is also a good idea to try to avoid expecting outcomes too soon. If a gallery likes your work, it may still take them a year or more to offer you a show. Most galleries plan their programme up to two years in advance, so even if a conversation has been started it could take a long time to conclude. Try not to get too disheartened if a gallery approaches you but then the contact diminishes, as this isn't necessarily out of the norm.

Contacting the director/curator through their personal channels should also always be avoided. It may seem like a surefire way to have your message seen, but this approach is much more likely to have the opposite effect to the one you were hoping for. It can come across as aggressive and invasive, two feelings that you don't want associated with your name. The fact that you often need to wait for galleries or curators to contact you may not be what you want to hear, but when done correctly it is possible to *make yourself discoverable.* By this we mean that while most galleries won't allow you to go to them, there are ways to encourage the galleries to come to you.

While you wait for the galleries to come knocking, strive to create a network of artists with whom you can collaborate, sharing resources and advice. Although galleries tend not to respond too well to direct approaches from artists, recommendations from *other* artists they are already working with are likely to be much more fruitful. It's a cruel psychology, but appearing too keen can put people off. It is always better to make yourself *visible,* but to allow the gallery to do the chasing.

In addition to venturing out to open studios and DIY shows in artist-led spaces, gallerists often look to the artists they already represent for tips on which other artists are making exciting work and, as always, keep an eye on whose work is being shared on social media by artists whose opinions they value. Therefore the backing of your peers can be invaluable. You never know whose career will take a great leap forward next, and so some of the artists you collaborate with now may be in a position to recommend you to someone who may be able to influence your career later on. The success of one's contemporaries often positively influences the careers of their network, too. Galleries and collectors will probably not be that receptive to your advances, but other artists might be. If you offer your support and your enthusiasm to people whose work you love, talking about and sharing their works, visiting their shows and helping them out in whatever ways you are able, they will probably do the same for you too.

To summarize, it may seem disheartening to learn that there aren't really that many avenues for you to contact galleries, and the idea of having to wait for them to contact you can make it feel as if it will never happen. Instead, don't see this revelation as a negative thing. Artists contacting galleries just isn't generally the way things tend to work, so instead of wasting your time amassing rejection after rejection and taking the ego hits that these can inflict, submit where applicable, and follow the guidelines above to maximize your chances of galleries directly approaching you. Instead of feeling dejected by this status quo, try to work within the established frameworks rather than becoming frustrated by them. Also, consider starting something yourself in the meantime, as this can lead to many opportunities in the future. Galleries will often take this as a sign that an artist is hard-working and driven, and isn't afraid to put themselves out there for something they want. These are all signs that you will continue to develop your work and your career in the long term and show that as good as your work may be now, it will be even stronger in the future.

What Galleries Want

The wants of galleries are a lot less complex than they may seem. Similarly to Maslow's hierarchy of needs,* these range from the most basic (continued survival) to the more fulfilling (originality). By outlining some of these here, we hope to help artists understand galleries better: to see them as living, breathing organisms that have worries and insecurities in the same way that we individuals do.

Sometimes, galleries are seen as faceless corporations that care only about sales, and while sales are important, galleries often have most of the same needs and desires as artists themselves. Many galleries are operated by a small team of passionate and driven individuals who sincerely care about the work and the artist they are showing. It is true that they need sales to survive, and can often be quite focused on them. But this is no different from any artist who relies purely on their work to survive. In many ways, the ability for a gallery to sustain itself can be more difficult than it might appear, as with limited space and time in which to host exhibitions (most galleries will hold around six to twelve yearly in their permanent space, and perhaps a few fairs or external projects on the side), the

---

* Maslow's hierarchy of needs is a psychological theory that organizes human needs into a pyramid with the most basic needs (for example food, shelter, sleep) at the bottom and the more advanced needs (respect from others, personal growth) at the top. Each of the most basic needs must be fulfilled before any higher needs can be met, and the most fulfilled people are those who have fulfilled every level of needs in turn.

need to make enough money to survive can preclude their ability to take too many risks. If a show doesn't sell, that shortfall needs to be made up from somewhere, and this can put extra pressure on future shows if they are also needed to fill a void left by an unsuccessful one.

We at Delphian are very lucky, as the way we operate allows for much more freedom than most other galleries. As we don't have any permanent staff, nor a permanent space, our monthly outgoings are quite low. However, they are still substantial, as galleries always must account for website and hosting costs, app and software subscriptions, accounting and a multitude of other services, which can all be quite costly. For this reason, we can afford to take larger risks and even do shows that we know will lead to us losing money, like our annual open call, from which we do not take a percentage of sales, instead covering all the costs ourselves. Not all galleries are able to operate like this, though. When galleries like Delphian exist, it can seem as if other galleries that don't have the same free-doms are exploitative of the artists they represent. To show how that isn't the case, we thought we'd explain some of the real-life concerns that galleries have from month to month.

All galleries need some kind of income to be able to operate. Rent, bills and staff salaries must all be paid. If none of these are met, the gallery will be forced to close. It is true that nomadic galleries (like Delphian) do not have a permanent site, but galleries still need space to exhibit and in those cases they must hire them or partner with other galleries. Some rely on sales to make an income to be able to pay for all these outgoings, but others rely on grants or charity.

It is all well and good having a space, some staff and some art, but you still need someone to come and see it. There can be no sales without an audience, and with no sales there can be no gallery. Once all the basic needs are met, galleries need to be spoken about. This helps people to choose to come and visit, makes artists want to exhibit with them, and helps them build their standing in the wider art world. This can take the form of press and reviews, as well as digital coverage such as on social media.

Galleries, like artists, want to develop. They want to expand, progress and evolve with their artists. In the same way that artists want to develop their output, so do galleries. No gallery wants to show only artists that everyone else is exhibiting, and many want to discover new and exciting talent to bring to the world stage. Ultimately, galleries often have many of the same worries that artists do. Having an understanding of these can help us to recognize why they make the decisions they make, and work in ways that are beneficial for all parties. Many of these concerns are difficult to address and the pursuit of solutions to them will drive most of the decisions the gallery makes. While artists may believe that all they need to take their careers to the next level is a gallery to 'take a chance' on them, unfortunately many galleries cannot afford to take risks when their continued survival is on the line. It may seem like galleries have nothing to lose and everything to gain, but the continued pressures of rent, bills and the other needs we have listed previously compound month by month. If one show doesn't sell well, the gallery's outgoing for that month don't decrease, they just need to find money to fill that shortfall from future shows, and the pressure grows and grows. On top of that are the needs for consistency, evolution, and public interest that may direct their decision-making too, so as artists its important to try and appreciate some of these pressures when approaching galleries, especially if the response received isn't what we might have hoped.

Proving Your Value

Self-belief is obviously essential in the pursuit of a career in the arts; it is almost impossible to succeed without it. With a few years of experience behind you and work you strongly believe in, it can be a hard knock to your confidence if you feel that no galleries are giving you or your work the chance it deserves.

Ultimately, strong work often isn't enough, and there are other things that galleries need to see before they start offering you opportunities. To an outsider, it can look like success happens overnight, but most artists work for many, many years before making their way into commercial galleries. Emerging artists may expect galleries to 'take a chance' on them. However, what this fails to recognize is that galleries are businesses, often only a few failed shows away from closure, and cannot afford to take many risks.

In this chapter, we will outline some things that galleries may need to see before they consider working with an artist. All of these take time, and in the development of an art career many artists unconsciously achieve all of the below by exhibiting in places like cafes and bars, taking part in craft fairs or art markets, entering open calls, engaging with the art world online, self-initiating projects, and sticking at it through all of its ups and downs.

The first thing a gallery needs to see is a passion for creativity and a drive to succeed. If they are going to consider putting their reputation, resources and time on the line to help you succeed, they need to see you doing the same for yourself. They need to see proof that you are obsessed with your practice, that it is something that you cannot abandon, and that you have the fortitude to push on through all the highs and lows of your career. No gallery is going to want to work with you if they can't be certain that you will still be working a year or two from now. Artists who aren't continually trying to find ways to experiment and develop their work often don't progress, and the progression of your practice is important. Repetitive work becomes old news very quickly, and this ability to drive your work forward consistently takes time.

The next thing a gallery looks for is sales potential. For artists, sales start slow and they start small. Many begin by selling things here and there to people they know and building up from there. But if you can build your sales until they reach a point at which a gallery could take over, this is going to make it a lot easier for them to invest in you. Your first gallery shouldn't vastly increase your prices overnight, though, so you should expect to build your sales up independently for quite a while (see 'Selling Your Work', p. 150, for more information).

Using the proper materials is an essential part of this. In order to sell, the work needs to be high-quality, but if you aren't selling much it can be hard to constantly spend your money on premium materials. There are many areas where you can cut corners if necessary, but working with substandard materials often leads to substandard work. Pre-stretched canvases are a good example of this. They are cheap and convenient, and so they are the obvious choice for early-career artists who need to be conscious of their outgoings so that they can still make work. This is, of course, fine on the surface but becomes an issue when the possibility for sales is introduced. If anyone is going to pay a significant amount of money for something, it needs to be well made.

While cheaper materials can encourage freedom and experimentation, which are essential to the development of your practice, this comes at the cost of quality (pre-stretched canvases, for example, are often flimsy, thin and prone to warping) and dissuades sales. It takes time to reach a point where the work necessitates higher-quality materials. If you are still very early on in your career and your works are very affordable (or don't yet sell at all) then using surfaces like pre-stretched shop-bought canvases isn't necessarily a problem, but this should be reassessed once your prices creep higher and you start selling more works.

Alongside this consideration about the quality of your materials, you need to develop the ability to take an objective view of your work and ensure that you are highly critical of your output. Many early-career artists fall into the trap of taking a scattergun approach and not applying strict quality controls when deciding what work is seen and what isn't. It is, of course, essential to experiment as much as possible, but the line between what is an example of experimentation and what is a finished artwork needs to be rigorous and non-emotional. Make sure that the work you put out into the world (both in physical exhibitions *and* on social media) is the best representation of yourself and your abilities. Not everything you make needs to be shown and if you are more selective, you have more control over how your work is perceived.

Many early-career artists can feel disheartened when they see their contemporaries achieving success, and don't understand why it may not be happening for them. Galleries will often say that good work is all that matters, and this is true to some extent. However, the points listed above are equally important factors in the development of your career. Galleries can't afford to take too many chances, so will often wait until most of these things have been achieved before they will consider working with an artist. Much of this is possible through conscious effort, but all of it takes time.

That said, and despite it being the aim of most early-career artists, being in too much of a rush to work with a gallery can have some negative impacts. Experimentation is key when developing an art career, and artists should endeavor to try as many things as possible at the beginning of their career. Signing with a gallery too soon can place undue pressure on you to work in a way that isn't natural, or to continue to create the same kind of works you were making when the gallery showed interest, even if it isn't the right thing for your practice. If this is the case, the work or medium might get repetitive and tired before long, and that early success can fade quickly. It is also possible that the sales just won't be there to justify this quick success. If sales don't materialize, or do but soon dry up, the gallery may drop you after one or two unsuccessful shows and then be reluctant to work with you again. Slow or non-existent sales are noticed by other galleries and collectors too, and this is a very visible indication that your career isn't quite there yet.

Hopefully, in this short chapter, we have elucidated how you can get your career to a point at which galleries are fighting to work with you. If they aren't showing interest yet, then don't worry. In the early days of your career, you should be trying to exhibit in as many experimental and varied locations as possible to gain experience and get your name out there as much as you can. Take part in artist-led shows, or curate some yourself in whatever space you can get hold of and engage with other artists both in the real world and online. Most crucially, though, use this time to experiment with your work and develop it until it reaches a stage at which it is ready to be seen by the world.

Why Others Are Getting Noticed

Comparing ourselves to our peers is rarely going to make us feel good, but it is also a hard thing to avoid. There are many reasons why one artist succeeds and another doesn't, and many of these are entirely out of anyone's control.

Hopefully, by drawing back the curtain a little and highlighting some of these reasons for success, this chapter will help you to identify the factors you can control and stop worrying about those you can't. A lot of anyone's success is down to luck, regardless of their field. This can be as simple as being in the right place at the right time or meeting the right person and being offered an opportunity as a result. Few people acknowledge this, because it can be seen to imply that the artist is undeserving of their success – that they didn't earn it. We are all granted strokes of luck here and there, and there's no shame in admitting it. It is, of course, impossible to improve your own luck by design, but what you *can* do is ensure that you are able to identify opportunities as they arise and be confident enough to grab them when they do. If your luck doesn't show up in times of need, be patient. It comes around eventually.

The old phrase 'It's not what you know, it's who you know' is definitely applicable in the arts. Knowing lots of people naturally means that a lot of people know you and, by extension, your work. This makes it much more likely you will be considered for opportunities. It is important not only to have a wide network, but also to nurture these relationships. Go to other artist's shows, visit galleries and support other's work whenever you can, online and off. This heightens the likelihood that your name will be fresh in someone's mind when they are considering artists to include in whatever project they are working on. It's almost impossible to overstate the importance of this point: the connections you make need to be genuine, and they need to be forged out of mutual support and encouragement, so find some artists whose work you like and show them (and the world) how great you think it is.

That said, it would be remiss of us not to acknowledge that nepotism is another reason why some artists succeed where others may not, and that knowing the *right* people can have a huge impact on the success of an artist's career. Too many artists avoid putting themselves out there because of shyness, lack of drive or the romantic belief that people will come to them if their work is good enough. Unfortunately, the work being great just isn't enough; you also have to get it, and yourself, out there. Utilize social media to its fullest, self-initiate projects and inhabit the area of the art world that you wish to get a break in. No one will seek you out unless they know you are there to begin with; if you avoid stepping into the spotlight then you must expect that you will forever remain in the shadows.

Another reason that an artist may get noticed is because their work is tapping into current trends. Chasing them is fraught with risks, though, and changing your work to fit the style that is popular right now should be avoided. Trends are fleeting, so if something is on trend now, it probably won't be in the near future. If you are always chasing, you will always be behind. Instead of trying to make work in the style of what is popular at the time, make what is authentically yours. This way you won't have to change it again when something else becomes popular. Not all artists whose work conforms to current trends are making this kind of work *because* it is the fashionable style, but rather because it was authentically theirs to begin with.

There is a balance to be struck, though, and while you should not chase trends, stagnation can be equally damning. The most exciting work evolves and develops over time as a result of experimentation, self-critique and a sincere passion for the process of making. Your work should keep improving, and the way to ensure that this happens is to be constantly questioning yourself about it, asking yourself questions like, 'What is the next step, and how do I get my work there?' Often you won't have answers to these questions immediately, and so experimentation is key. If you can look at two works that were made with a significant time in between and the most recent one doesn't seem more interesting, developed or revolutionary, you may want to change things up a bit. Always strive for the next development in your work because even if you think it is really strong right now, what comes next is likely to be stronger.

Starting Something Yourself

The benefits of starting something yourself cannot be overstated. It is something that has never been easier and doesn't have to take up as much of your time as you might think. Delphian was the result of two artists deciding to start something themselves and has now become something far larger than either of us ever imagined. There's no reason why you couldn't do something similar (or bigger, even) if you have that aspiration.

Many artists desire an outlet to make things happen themselves, turning to curation, writing and other projects that are connected to the art world but not intrinsic to their art practice. These artists often then see the benefits of this activity in their work as a result, although not always in an obvious and tangible way.

It is no secret that networking is a huge part of being an artist, and it is clear that those who develop this skill have an easier time succeeding than those who neglect it. When you make something possible for others, you contribute to their success, and this altruism almost always comes back around in some form. Whether or not you believe in the concept of karma, it is clear that the more people you help, the more they are going to be inclined to help you out, too. Being someone who makes things happen is also great for your reputation. Showing that you have initiative, the ability to follow your ideas through, and the fearlessness that makes this possible can increase your visibility and dependability in the eyes of others. If you have curated a DIY show or launched an online publication, for example, you are showing that you have been able to pull something interesting together with little to no resources, and this doesn't go unnoticed. One of the largest shows we have curated to date was offered to us because we were the only gallery that sprang to mind when the gallery director asked, 'Who is crazy enough to say yes to curating a show of this size with only a week's notice?'

CURATION

The benefits of curating cannot be overstated. Engaging in the curation of even a small show can do wonders for your own practice and how you approach showing your work in the future. It is immensely useful to see behind the curtain: to understand what goes into the organization of an exhibition and learn what galleries are doing on your behalf.

Curation essentially means 'the arranging of objects', and that definition does a good job of showing how much scope for interpretation there is. We have seen exhibitions hosted in people's houses, in bars and cafes, in public spaces such as fields and streets, in abandoned buildings, and almost anywhere else you can imagine. Just because most exhibitions we encounter are in traditional gallery-style settings doesn't mean that they all have to be. In fact, the more experimental you are in selecting your 'gallery space', the more memorable the show will be. If you decide to try your hand at curation, think about what is available and how you can utilize the uniqueness of the situation to make something interesting that people won't have seen before. Instead of trying to make your cafe exhibition look like a show at the National Gallery, celebrate the environment you are working with and integrate the show into the space in as experimental and interesting a way as you can. An exhibition is a collection of artworks by a heterogeneous group of artists, often making works from their own unique positionality and with differing interests and incentives. As the curator, you become the one unifying force that brings these disparate elements together, and by doing so, you create something entirely new. Try to think of any show you curate as being an artwork in its own right. Approach it as a creative act and try to express yourself through how you collect and arrange the works. Use it as a platform to make statements or raise questions, and allow the viewer the space to interpret their way to their own answer.

WRITING

Art writing or critique can be published online for free using a blog or website incredibly easily. If you have an interest in this, the website can be used alongside social media to create an innovative online presence for all things written. Interviews, theoretical or historical essays, artist-selected playlists, reviews, fiction, poetry, opinion pieces, round-ups and even content such as recipes can all be used to explore art and creativity alongside your own art practice. This type of platform is incredibly cheap to get up and running and is something you can invite your friends and contemporaries to contribute to. It's a great way to raise talking points that are important to you and to initiate discussions on topics that may not be spoken about elsewhere.

If it is shyness that is holding you back, consider giving the platform or website a name of its own until you find your voice and develop the confidence to be the face of it. This anonymity also makes it easier to abandon the practice entirely if it turns out it isn't for you, with nothing lost but experience gained.

Whatever you decide to do, try to celebrate your own uniqueness and the situation in which you find yourself. Don't try to find ways of forcing whatever resources you have available into being a poor facsimile of the typical exhibitions or publications you are inspired by; instead, try to be as experimental as you are in your artwork. The most crucial thing here is that you are truly passionate about what it is you are doing. Try to create the types of shows, platforms or publications that *you* would love to see, and if you do so you will have no trouble in attracting an audience.

The Exhibition Checklist

Eventually you will reach a point in your career when you decide you want to start showing your work. Many early-career artists start off by exhibiting in places like cafes and project spaces, and if you choose to do so you will be responsible for practically everything involved in hosting an exhibition yourself. Once you begin showing with galleries they should handle most of the organization for you, but until that point, whenever you host your own exhibition you can use this chapter to ensure that you have everything ready ahead of time and that no nasty surprises arise when it is too late to address them.

PROMOTING THE EXHIBITION

The first step is to prepare high-resolution, well-lit photographs of your work. You will need these for social media, the sales catalogue and the press release, so taking them in your studio as soon as the works are complete is a good way to tick things off as soon as possible. The background should be plain and white, and the border that is visible around the artwork itself should be uniform.

Another useful step is to make a note of the title, dimensions, materials, price and year of each work for the catalogue to save yourself time later on. If you are being extra-organized you might also want to make a note of the weight of each work, as this will help you get shipping estimates should any of them be sold.

In addition to creating a sales catalogue and press release, you may wish to create physical invitations to the show. Invites are a great way to get people to visit your exhibition, especially if they are targeted towards people directly rather than sent out en masse, and the more personal these are the greater the likelihood that they will be successful. One thing we have done in the past is produce high-quality printed invites onto which we have hand-written a personal message and delivered them in a wax-sealed envelope. This kind of approach (while a little more time-consuming to produce) definitely creates a lasting impact.

Printed posters and flyers are less essential now that social media is so widely used, but they can still be an effective way to promote your exhibition, especially to people who may not know of you or who may be in the local area. Image-led posters and flyers attract the most attention, but they should still detail salient information about the show. There is no need for the full press release here, but they should include your name, the show title, the dates and address, and a website or social media link where they can find more information if they want to. A QR code is an effective way of providing easy access to this extra information but is not a substitute for the above-mentioned details.

You may not have many contacts in the press at this stage, but it can't hurt to put in some time researching suitable publications such as magazines, blogs and cultural commentators to invite them to the show. When you contact these people you can include the press release, but try to make it come across like a personal invitation to the show rather than something that you have sent out to everyone in your contacts. Include some images of the work in your email, with instructions to get in touch if they need any more information. It's good to look for publications that have posted similar exhibitions in the past, that are based in the area where the show is taking place or that have some kind of connection to the work itself.

You will want to promote your exhibition ahead of time on social media. In-progress or detail shots of the work can be a really good way to provoke interest in the show without giving too much away. Some mystery should be retained so as to encourage people to visit the show, so try not to share too many photos of full, finished artworks before you open.

SELLING WORK

When someone is considering buying an artwork, their decision is based on many factors. Some of these you will not be able to influence (for example, they may be weighing up whether to buy an artwork or to save the money for a holiday), but there are some that you can. What is most important, is that everything involved in the sales process, from the potential buyer's initial discovery of the exhibition to the final purchase and delivery of the work, feels as professional and as comfortable as possible. Below is a checklist for some of the structures you should have in place to facilitate these transactions.

The small red dot is the universal symbol of a sold artwork. These stickers can be picked up at most stationery stores, and when placed upon the wall besides the artwork they let everyone know that a work has been bought. The more red dots on the wall, the more successful the show seems be in the minds of potential buyers, and they can serve to introduce some immediacy in their decision of whether or not to purchase a work.

The exhibition catalogue is essentially a document that details the works included in the show and provides important information, such as the dimensions, size, title and medium of each piece. Most catalogues also include the price of each work – as knowing this detail immediately without having to ask has been proven to increase the likelihood of sales. People often feel intimidated to ask for the prices and may choose not to, so as to avoid any pushy sales messages afterwards. The best way to encourage sales is to make it as clear and as easy for people to buy as possible, so if they can buy through the catalogue itself and pay then and there, they are less likely to forget or change their minds. For self-organized shows especially, this is a great approach. If this is your first ever exhibition then you may not yet have a list of collectors to send the catalogue to, but this is something you are going to want to start compiling as soon as enquiries start coming in. One thing you can do to start this process is to mention on your social media that the catalogue will be going out soon, and that anyone who wants to receive it should give you their email address. Keep a spreadsheet of all of these and add to it every time you are contacted by someone. Then you can contact these people whenever you launch a show or release a new body of work. Don't overdo it, though: remember that not everyone needs to hear about everything that you are working on all the time, so save these emails for updates that really count.

If you are lucky there may be some interest from visitors in purchasing your work. To facilitate this you will want to make it easy for everyone to see the prices of all the works. Larger galleries may keep this information hidden and only give it out if requested, but if you are hosting your own exhibition that is less necessary. Instead, have a stack of well-laid-out price lists on a table or plinth that people can pick up and read at their leisure. These should have all of the work details included, as well as a small photo or number that helps them identify which details apply to which artwork. There should be enough of these that every person can take one home with them, and they should have your contact details at the bottom. It may seem counterintuitive to have contact details on something that the viewers will be given at the show, but sometimes people may want to think about it for a while before purchasing. If they are able to take this price list home with them they will not only have all the artwork details at hand, but also they will know how to contact you if they do decide to buy.

Some people prefer sticky labels with details and prices that are affixed on the wall next to the works instead of a printed price list, but as well as disrupting the view of the works, these also lack the added benefits of printed price lists outlined above. If you do decide to go this route, they should always be small, well designed and printed rather than handwritten. Some galleries use QR codes in place of price lists or labels, but not everyone is able to scan them and it is possible that they won't always work. If you do use a QR code, it would be prudent to have printed price lists on hand also.

At the exhibition, you are likely to encounter many visitors who have not seen your work before or do not follow you on social media. They may be local to the area, know the gallery or space you are exhibiting in, or have been brought by a friend. To take full advantage of this new crowd that your work is reaching, it is important to collect their contact details if you can. The best way to do this is to have a mailing list sign-up sheet somewhere visible so that any interested parties can write down their names and email addresses, which you then add to your mailing list afterwards. They can then be contacted whenever you have a new show or release new artwork: as they have been interested in the past, they are likely to be so again. Try not to send too many emails to this mailing list though: no more than a few times a year would be the optimal amount, as people can get annoyed if they are too frequent, and a significant amount of unsubscribes or non-opens of a mailing list will harm its future reach.

Most exhibition openings provide some kind of complimentary drinks so that the night is more of an event. This provides the lubrication that makes people more comfortable mingling and networking with others they may not have met before, and openings with no refreshments are often left as soon as people get thirsty. It's always a good idea to provide beer or wine, as well as something non-alcoholic for any non-drinkers or children who may attend. In some countries, it is encouraged that visitors bring their own drinks, and sometimes people will ask for voluntary donations for those that are provided. However, if at all possible, making these refreshments completely free for any visitors will always go down well, and potentially set you apart from those not doing so.

Many artists also like to have something available at the exhibition that is more affordable than the original works, and so many opt for a limited-edition print to release at the opening. These should always be high quality and true to the work they have been created from. Prints are much easier to 'impulse buy', so it is always a good idea to let people take them home on the night. For this, you will need suitable packing materials such as tissue paper, tape and print tubes or envelopes.

On the whole, your first self-hosted exhibition should be seen as a learning experience. It may feel unfamiliar and overwhelming at times, but the knowledge you receive from instigating a project like this yourself will be invaluable to you throughout your career. If you keep the above tips in mind it will be more than possible for you to host your own exhibition that feels professional, interesting and exciting.

The Edges of Identity

WINGSHAN

Wingshan is an artist and curator based in Nottingham, UK. Through her work, she emphasizes interaction and collectivity, bringing magical, decolonial and feminist methodologies from the theoretical realm into practice.

In a world where oppression is interconnected and intersected, the experiences of marginalized artists reveal both the unique and collective impact of these forces. As artists, we navigate a landscape shaped by our identities – whether these are rooted in ethnicity, gender identity, sexuality, class, disability or neurodivergency. Each of these identities brings its own challenges, but they also converge, creating a complex web of barriers that can dictate how we are seen, valued and heard in the art world.

This text emerges from a sense of impatience and disenchantment with a system that, despite the increased discourse of inclusion, still allows spaces intended for cultural expression to be dominated by those who do not share our lived experiences. Here I don't offer easy answers, but instead attempt to delve into the many layers that define our artistic journeys. I want to explore the intersections where our identities meet, the unique spaces we create in safety and the tension between these safe spaces and the public performance of making art and being an artist. How do we seek to connect with others artistically, hoping to be understood and not misinterpreted?

The journey of navigating these edges is fraught with moments of self-doubt and the constant pressure to conform. Yet within these very borderlands lies profound strengths – an ability to see the world from multiple perspectives, to create art that challenges norms and to speak truths that are often left unspoken. These are the qualities that make minority artists not only resilient, but also essential voices in the broader cultural conversation.

However, this journey is not without its toll. The ongoing shift between personal creation and public performance can be draining. There is a delicate balance between protecting the self and exposing it – between staying true to one's authentic voice, and navigating the expectations of the industry. We grapple with what to write in our artist biographies, for example, considering if our identities should narrowly define us, or worse, if we are attempting to profit off a wider struggle. Yet choosing to omit our identity markers can make it seem like we're ashamed of them, or that we are not showing solidarity with others who share similar backgrounds.

This tension is particularly heightened when opportunities arise that seem to offer us visibility and recognition but may come at the cost of our integrity. The fear of being reduced to a mere token of diversity is ever present. Navigating opportunities that are closed to certain identities means constantly wondering if these offers seek to exploit us.

Sometimes you have to seize the opportunity and move forward. There are many challenges we might face, and we all deserve to meet our needs. Yet this can come at the risk of entering harmful exchanges that affect our wellbeing or even cause harm to others. If you find yourself in this situation, it could be helpful to consider the following questions: who is asking for our work? Why are they inviting us in particular? What aftercare will they provide once the work is out in the world? Are they genuinely committed to better representation at decision-making levels, or is this merely a superficial nod to inclusivity? Will this work reach the right audiences?

The phrase 'nothing about us, without us' resonates here. It's a guiding tenet in all the work I do. Since first hearing this I've heard it echoed in various settings, from Pride marches to museum board meetings. These things do catch on. Hope always prevails.

As a disabled artist and arts worker, I have an access rider.* If you are differently abled, consider writing a document to share with organizations you work with that outlines your needs. This can also include notes on further reading for making their spaces or events more accessible. It is always a good idea to signpost resources to organizations.

Writing an access rider can feel challenging in a similar way to writing an artist biography. There is an ever-present discomfort at naming the details of oneself to strangers. Some artists create 'dark bios' that are meant to be shared only with close friends, family and a select few others. These bios allow them to express themselves honestly, without the need to conform to the jargon of funding bodies or the

* There are several online guides to help you write an access rider of your own, if you decide you would like to.

buzzwords of the art world. Writing these deeply personal texts can be incredibly freeing, but it can also be frightening to strip away the performative aspects of our identities and reveal our true selves. It makes us wonder: do we still recognize who we are beneath all the layers we've built up?

Writing a dark bio is a nice exercise to explore what parts of us we keep hidden and what parts of ourselves and our histories we wish to reveal. It enables us to decide how to remember and reclaim our stories when our histories have been erased or only exist in ways shaped by a white, male-dominated, able-bodied gaze.

Over the years my approach has been to embrace this messiness. The best stories and culture are passed down with room to evolve and adapt into our present. The most powerful types of histories and rituals are ones that can transform our futures. My practice, like my identity, is a melting pot that refuses to be defined in reductive terms. I honour myself and my people by choosing the ways I speak and to whom I speak my truth.

We must resist falling into the capitalist trap of valuing our artwork output in superficial numbers of sales, audience attendance and online reach. Impact is emotional. It is long-term. It is difficult to measure. The most meaningful work can be done in small circles.

On the topic of hidden spaces, I am also a strong advocate for the whisper networks that occur between people who share the same values. Cathartically sharing the good, the bad and the ugly of your experiences is a powerful tool in a strategic approach that I like to call 'radical truth-telling'.

In circles where trust and solidarity have been established, this is a form of resistance. It allows artists to share vital information and warn each other of potential pitfalls, spaces and people to avoid. In these intimate moments, we can also celebrate successes in ways that the broader art world may not understand or appreciate. This is a form of empowerment: a way to reclaim agency in a system that often seeks to strip it away.

This industry is a place where dreams are realized, but it can be tough out there, especially for those who are not adequately represented. The importance of alliances cannot be overstated. Email someone you admire and request a meeting over coffee. Go to events programmed by individuals you know you will connect with.

Building strategic relationships with others who share similar values and concerns is crucial for navigating the art world without losing oneself. These alliances provide not only practical support, but also a sense of community and shared purpose. They reinforce the idea that while each artist's experience is unique, there is strength in friendship and collective action.

Through doing this I have been introduced to networks and communities that have helped me feel true belonging. It required research (and a little bit of bravery) to reach out, set up and join group chats that have since turned into dim sum, research collectives, poetry nights and more. We gather, eat, share and create together. There is so much potential for joy in collaboration.

What I suggest here is a balance of retreat and celebration. Take care of your needs first so that you have the strength and resources to help others effectively. Our identities, in all their complexity, are not a burden but a gift. They are the source of our unique perspectives, our creative power, and our ability to envision and build a better, more just world.

As we continue to navigate these edges of identity, let us remember the importance of asking the right questions; of advocating for ourselves and for others; of finding and creating spaces where we can share our stories. Let us hold onto hope, knowing that each step we take, each piece of art we create and each truth we tell contributes to a larger movement towards inclusivity, equity and understanding.

The Artist's Toolkit

Below is a list of resources that you can prepare to make your career run smoother later on. It is much better to have these ready for when you need them than to discover the need when it is too late. Some are more important or useful than others. Some you will need often, and others more rarely. If you have them all prepared ready for when you need them, there will be no scary surprises down the line. We have detailed how to create the most complex of these in separate chapters, so here is a short list of what you may need at some point in your career.

SOCIAL MEDIA

As we've covered fairly extensively already in this book, your social media is now the first place your work is likely to be discovered by the majority of people who come across it. It can be much more fluid and informal than something like your website or portfolio, and you can (if you wish) get across a little more of your personality here. You can include further details about yourself and your life, as people often want to learn more about the person behind the art, and this is the most relevant platform to show it. You need to invest time and effort in this because it is by far the most valuable marketing tool you have available to you. It's also free.

BUSINESS CARDS

Not all artists have these any more, and if what you make is visual then something more like a postcard might be more suitable. Handing over something physical that the receiver may hold onto can sometimes be more valuable than writing down your website on a piece of paper, or having them write down your social media handle. It is also a good visual record of your work that the receiver can view without you all getting your phones out, which can lead to further distractions. All of your contact details, website address and social media handles should be included. A postcard also has the added benefit of being something that people may stick directly on their wall or even frame.

WEBSITE

Despite the power of social media as a first port of call, a website is still essential. Here you can include resources like video, documents and press releases, as well as high-quality images of your best work. It should be updated regularly, have links to your social media, email and mailing list, and be easily navigable. Keep this much more professional than your social media, and include your full CV and artist statement either as text blocks on an 'about' page or similar, or as downloadable documents.

CV

This is a list of all the relevant events that have been part of your artistic career to date, including all the information you might expect, such as the shows you have been in or clients you have worked with, and educational background. (See 'Writing Your Artist CV', p.130, for further details.)

ARTIST'S STATEMENT

Elsewhere in this book, we go into further details on how to compose one of these, so we will be brief here. This is a document that serves as a roadmap with which the viewer can learn more about you the artist and what you are attempting to do in your work. (See 'Writing Your Artist Statement', p. 134, for further details.)

STUDIO PORTRAITS

This may sound like something that isn't essential, but you will be asked for these often. Trying to organize taking one at short notice can be difficult and these should be updated as your work evolves. Try to include at least part of your work or workspace in the background, as this usually leads to a more striking photograph. Wear whatever you usually would in the studio and try to appear as natural and comfortable in your surroundings as you can. These are great for inclusion on your website and social media too.

PORTFOLIO

This is a digital document (physical portfolios are rarely necessary these days) that can be sent out to potential clients, galleries or buyers. You might want to have multiple versions (for example, the one you send to galleries should include only your strongest work, including work that you have sold, while the one you would send to potential buyers should only include work that is available for purchase), but each should be very well designed, with simple and non-distracting formatting and high-quality photos of your work. Crops and detail shots are good here, but in-progress photographs should perhaps be reserved for your social media. Your portfolio always needs to be as up-to-date as possible.

EMAIL/MAILING LIST

A professional-sounding email address (your name works best) is a given, and a mailing list is a good way to keep yourself fresh in the minds of those who are interested in your work. Compile this well, and send it out sparingly. (See p. 106 for more information.)

SALES SPREADSHEET

This is a document in which you keep track of all of your previous buyers,* and all those who enquired about purchasing something but for whatever reason didn't. As explained elsewhere in this book, those listed in this

---

* A cautionary note on this point: when you sell through a second party (i.e. a gallery, dealer or shop), they won't always be able to share the personal details of buyers with you. In some instances, this may even be against the law, so if they aren't forthcoming with this information it's usually because they know their responsibilities towards their customers and won't share their details without explicit permission being granted.

spreadsheet are by far the most likely to be interested in future work, so having their details close at hand will be useful.

This document is an invaluable resource that will make your life much easier later down the line. You will always wish you had started it sooner, so anticipate that future frustration now and get to work on it.

The Ruinous Effect of the Empty Page

Almost all artists start their careers with an intense fear of talking about their work. It is true that a picture is worth a thousand words, and so when we try to explain our artwork using words, we are attempting the impossible. In fact, the very reason we express ourselves with images is because we simply *cannot* say the same in words. Even harder than speaking about our work is writing about it.

Unfortunately, as you progress through your career as an artist you will find that sometimes this is impossible. Below we have provided a framework for how this often daunting task can be approached. (It also applies to the fear of the blank canvas too, so in most instances the word 'writing' can be substituted for 'painting', and 'page' for 'canvas'.)

When beginning any piece of writing we can often be overwhelmed by possibility to a ruinous extent. The perfection of a pristine blank page is hard to interrupt if we think too much about what we are doing. If we expect the first word on this page to be perfect, to not destroy the limitless potential the emptiness contains, then we will never put pen to paper.

Think of the last time you had to do a piece of writing – an essay or similar – and how impossible it felt to start. Trying to begin with the first line of the introduction feels almost impossible and so is rarely the best approach. The best thing to do when beginning to write is to ignore the introduction until the very end – embrace the journey of discovery this will take you on. First comes the ideas generation stage: the research and the pursuit of inspiration. The first step is to read about what inspires you. Note-taking is essential, so highlight everything that sparks off an idea, record where you found this nugget of information or imagery so that you know where to find it later *and move on*. When you come to take notes ensure that you do this in your own words: don't copy things down exactly as they were in the source material, as doing so forces your brain to digest and understand this information rather than just memorize it momentarily. Writing things down in your own words cements the idea in your own mind in a much more lasting way than copying, so avoid that at all costs. If possible, do this note-taking by hand too, because the haptic process of writing by hand contributes to even deeper memorization and understanding than typing it.

Once this research is underway, it's important to record all the information somehow, without worrying about form until much later. A good way to think about this is to call it a 'mind dump', for what you are doing is essentially vomiting everything you've learned and the connections your mind has made onto the page. All concerns about grammar, legibility (to an extent) and linear narrative should be abandoned in favour of speed and efficiency. Your goal here should be volume over quality because it's important to capture all of this knowledge before it is forgotten or pushed out of your mind by other new and exciting information. Write down every quote, phrase, word or sentence that comes to mind. Include the names of other artists or artworks, films, TV shows, books and video games that have a connection to your work. Then try to say what it is about these that interests you, even if what you write down doesn't have an identifiable connection to how your work appears.

This probably won't be a particularly readable body of text yet, and that's okay. More than okay, in fact, because it means that you have followed the guidelines and haven't wasted any precious time or effort tweaking what will be edited beyond recognition in the next step anyway.

Following this mind-dump phase comes the edit: the laborious, but massively constructive, edit. Here is where the magic happens, because everything you have learned and understood becomes coherent. Highlight words, draw lines between ideas that connect and try to make some sense of the madness. Take out and reorder parts that naturally go together until new sentences start to emerge in your mind and paragraphs begin to form. Use this approach to collect sentences that can be rewritten and edited with other related ones in mind, and eventually, these blocks of text will find their way into an order that makes sense.

This framework can be applied to the creation of an artwork, too, interestingly, because many of the challenges that make it hard to begin an artwork are the same. Luckily, so are the solutions. Editing is transformative and is the only real way to mitigate the fear of starting. We don't expect the first few marks we make on the canvas (or the first few words we write down) to be the work of a genius, and trust that through continued consideration and work, through editing and tweaking early impressions, we can arrive at something that is a product of the journey we were taken on in its creation. The beauty of artistic creation is that no one but yourself gets to decide when something is complete, which means that you have almost unlimited scope with which to continue developing a work until you're happy with it.

When we realize this, we free ourselves from the constraints imposed by the expectation that everything needs to start out well. If you were to have seen the first draft of this book and compare it with the one you hold in your hands now, we're sure you'd know exactly what we mean.

Writing about Your Work

For most of us, being equally articulate both visually and verbally is a challenge. While we may feel confident expressing ourselves through our work, trying to describe or justify that work with words often doesn't come as naturally. This is a discomfort we will have to work through often, as exhibition texts and press releases become more and more essential the further you progress in your career. While it is true that galleries might write these themselves (or commission someone to write them on their behalf), they will still always want some direction from you as to what your art is trying to achieve.

The more information about your work you are able to put into words the better, as it is much easier to misconstrue an abstract gesture upon canvas say, than it is a paragraph of text. While it is true that everyone will find their own individual meaning in the work, it is often useful for them to hear it from the artist's perspective too. The more detail you can give to the gallery or writer the better, as this not only helps them in conveying your intentions in the official gallery text, but also enables them to get a better feel for your work, so they will feel more confident in discussing it with enquirers. It can also help to avoid any misunderstandings that may arise if they are discussing your work based upon their own interpretations of what it means, rather than your intentions. Both of these perspectives are valid and interesting for the viewer to hear, but the two should not be conflated.

A good way to get started is to seek out interviews with other artists and pay special attention to how they describe their own work. Listen to the language they use and try to identify words that could also be applied to your own. Another option is to write about the work of other artists, as the comparative freedom that comes with writing about someone else can help to build your confidence and get your writing muscles into shape. When writing or talking about our own work, however, we should be discussing the intentions and inspirations, and not the interpretations. Don't tell the viewer what the work should mean in concrete terms. Each artwork will be interpreted differently by everyone who views it, and you have to let the viewer decide their own meaning. Essentially, an artwork has as many interpretations as it has viewers. What you can do, though, is tell them either what inspired the work or what ideas the work is exploring.

Below is a rough structure of how a gallery text or press release should be presented, although this can of course be suited to your purpose. There will be a lot of formal '[Gallery Name] is pleased to present ...' type information on there too, but as this is something that will differ from gallery to gallery and won't ever be the responsibility of the artist to write, we've chosen to omit it here.

After the title, location and other factual information has been provided, there will need to be at least a few paragraphs of text about you and your work that help the viewer to understand or interpret it. Galleries will often ask you to provide this and will use the important details to create a press release and exhibition text. For a solo show you will likely be more involved in this process than you might be for a group show comprising many artists, but the more accurate and detailed the information you provide them with, the less likely it is that your work will be misrepresented. Here is the order in which these elements are presented in such a document.

WHO Who you are, where you are from, and where you live and work now. You may choose to include other information such as your age, gender identity, racial identity or sexuality if these are intrinsic to the meaning of your work, but you shouldn't feel obliged to. (See 'The Edges of Identity, p. 108, for further details on this.)

WHAT What is the title and key medium(s) used in the show, what should the visitor expect to encounter and how will works appear? These are objective facts.

WHY What were your inspirations and intentions with the work, what is it about (for you) and why were you compelled to make it?

SO WHAT Why should the viewer care, what does this work do that hasn't been done before, why is it relevant now and what new insight does the work provide? Why is it *important*? Something we see often in the 'so what' section is meaningless exaggerated platitudes such as 'The show forces the viewer to question the nature of reality.' This is rarely the case, and so remarks like this are best omitted.

For much of the first section and part of the second, you will be able to repurpose the text you've already written for your artist statement. This will probably be the case for every exhibition going forward. However, you'll want to keep this updated as your career progresses and your work evolves. The same can also be said for your CV, website and portfolio.

After all of this, it is customary to include some career highlights or a copy of the artist's CV in a separate section, as well as a similar piece of text about the gallery itself. Again, this will differ from gallery to gallery and is usually something that they will produce.

THE 'FIVE WHYS'

Having to explain your work may fill you with fear at the mere suggestion, especially if you are near the beginning of your artistic journey. Most artists have no problem addressing *who* and *what* because these don't require much conceptual thinking. They deal with facts and so cannot be disagreed with. After this, though, you'll need to talk about *why* you make your work and what it might mean; this is where it becomes much harder. Explaining your work conceptually is an intimidating thing to do at the best of times, but if we develop some writing tools it becomes a lot easier.

When making work, some artists start with a concept or idea and then try to find a way of accurately conveying that message. Let's call this style of working *concept first*. Working like this can be very effective when done well, and those who work this way might have an easier time explaining their artwork than those who don't.

However, working intuitively and without a preconceived notion of what the artwork will be about is also entirely legitimate. We can refer to this style of working as *concept second*. Many artists rely on their subconscious when making, and don't try to inject any specific meaning into their work. They may create spontaneously or instinctively and then, when it is time to talk about their work, they may feel as if there isn't that much to say. That doesn't mean that the meaning isn't there: we just have to do a little bit more digging to find it.

If you are a concept second kind of artist, it might help to ask yourself a series of questions to determine why you made the subconscious decisions that you did. Below, we have outlined a framework of questioning known as the 'five whys'. If you make decisions instinctually, you can use a technique like the five whys to find deeper concepts to talk about when describing your work.

To show you how it is done, here is an imagined example of how Vincent van Gogh might have approached this exercise about his painting *The Starry Night*:

What did I do?
I painted the sky.

Why 1: Why did I paint the sky?
Because I wanted to capture my reality.

Why 2: Why did you want to capture your reality?
Because I find life difficult, and I want to express that.

Why 3: Why do you want to record this for others?
Because it might help them to understand themselves, to know that they aren't the only ones that feel this way.

Why 4: Why is it important to help others in your work?
Because I don't want others to feel isolated and lonely, like I do.

At this point, we don't need the fifth why, because the answer we have is already quite deep and interesting. If we talk about our work being the way it is because we are exploring the points mentioned above, we are talking about it in a deeper way that shows we are really considering what we are doing, and that we understand it well.

If we didn't get a satisfying answer from asking four or five whys, we can ask ourselves six or seven. Or we can start again and explore a different angle. For example:

What did I do?
I painted the sky with thick, expressive brushstrokes.

Why 1: Why are the brushstrokes thick?
Because they came out that way, naturally.

Why 2: Why did they come out that way, naturally?
Because I was feeling intense emotions at the time.

Why 3: What were those emotions?
Frustration, sadness, loneliness. I was scared and I was seeing things. (*This one became a what rather than a why, but the effect is the same.*)

Why 4: Why is it important that you paint during these times?
Because it helps me understand the world and to make sense of my emotions.

Why 5: Why is it important that you understand the world and make sense of your emotions?
Because if I didn't, I could not survive.

With this exercise, we can trick our subconscious into revealing its secrets – the reasons our mind made the instinctual decisions that it did. We might also use it to find potential interpretations of our work that we can discuss or describe, regardless of whether those were the things that inspired us to begin with.

Writing Your Artist CV

An artist CV is something that you will need at all stages of your artistic journey and can be difficult and time-consuming to create. In essence, an artist CV is a list of your professional achievements and experience to date. Crucially, it should not be written using the flowery, over-the-top language one might expect in a press release, but instead as a fairly dry list of achievements.

The first point you will want to state is your name, which is fairly self-explanatory. What should be noted, though, is that the name you use needs to be kept consistent. If you sometimes use a shortened version of your name, for example, you should decide which you want to go by professionally, and use that name everywhere. Brand recognition is key, and people won't naturally assume that two names they have seen written down are the same person, even if one is a short-form version of the other.

Everything listed here should be organized from the most recent at the top to the least recent at the bottom.

YOUR BIRTH DATE AND BIRTHPLACE

This is contestable. People will often want to know this information, but artists might sometimes decide that this isn't something they want to make public knowledge. Neither is the 'right way', but it is more common to include it than to omit it. If you are represented formally by a gallery you should mention who they are and in what location they represent you here.

YOUR CURRENT LOCATION

People always want to know this, as it can help them to understand or identify with you and your work. This also helps galleries and curators as they can factor shipping and delivery times into their scheduling.

EDUCATION

Where you studied, the grade achieved and when. If you have a lot of qualifications in very diverse fields, you may choose to only list those relevant to your artistic career. The highest level should be at the top. The more qualifications you receive, the less important it is to include the earliest ones. School- or college-level qualifications can be omitted if you have a degree, for example.

SELECTED EXHIBITIONS

For each show, list the title, gallery, location and date. The later you are in your career, the more edited you may want this list to be. If you are at the beginning of your career, list everything. If you have been exhibiting for a while and the list is long, trim it down or consider dividing it into separate solo, duo and group show sections, as the fewer artists there are in an exhibition with you, the more significant your contribution will be.

CURATED EXHIBITIONS

If you have curated any shows, list the title, gallery, location and date. If you like, you can also mention some of the artists involved.

AWARDS, GRANTS AND RESIDENCIES

If you have won any awards, open calls, residencies or other juried prizes that are connected to your artistic practice, list them here.

NOTABLE COLLECTIONS

If museums, large galleries or notable collections have bought your work, you may want to mention it here. Some private collections may not want this information made public, so it's always best to make sure it's okay when listing individuals by name. For each entry, detail the name of the collection, the city and the country – for example, MoMA, New York City, USA.

SPEAKING AND WRITING ENGAGEMENTS

This section can be used to list any lectures, panel discussions or recorded interviews you have been involved in, as well as any relevant teaching or writing experience you may have. For each entry, detail the title of the talk, course or prize; the hosting institution; the location and the date.

PRESS AND GALLERY MENTIONS

Here is where you can include either clickable links (in a digital document) or references to where such information can be found (in a printed document) to any press coverage you have received or a list of publications that have mentioned your work. You may also want to include links to any galleries that you are currently showing with or have shown with recently.

SAMPLE CV

[Name] Lives and works in [place name].
b.[birthplace], [year]

EDUCATION
Course, institution, [enrolment year]–[graduation year], grade achieved.

SOLO EXHIBITIONS
[*Title*, gallery, city, year]

SELECTED GROUP EXHIBITIONS
[*Title*, gallery, city, year]

CURATED EXHIBITIONS
[*Title*, gallery, city, year]

AWARDS, GRANTS AND RESIDENCIES
[Residency name, location, year]
[Award name, winner/shortlisted/longlisted, year]

NOTABLE COLLECTIONS
[Collection name, city, country]

SPEAKING AND WRITING ENGAGEMENTS
[Lecture title, hosting institution, course, year]
['Article title', *publication*, edition number, year]

PRESS AND GALLERY LINKS
[Exhibition title, gallery, location, year]
['Article title', *publication*, year]

Writing Your Artist Statement

Your artist statement is what interested parties will use to get a deeper understanding of you as an artist and the work that you make. It is usually included on your website and as an attachment to (or adapted to become) the press release for any exhibitions you may have. When written well, these invaluable texts will not only help others to understand your practice but also develop the language with which you talk about your work. Usually between 100 and 500 words in length, this document can be trimmed or expanded to suit many purposes and should be updated and edited regularly as your work evolves. Below, we have listed some of the most essential elements. However, it is important to note that this document is adaptable and should be shaped to fit your needs.

WHO YOU ARE — Including, but not limited to, where you are from, when you were born (although some choose to leave this out) and (if you like) why you started making art. This section gives the reader their first insight into who you are as a person and helps them to understand some of the context in which you make your work. You may also choose to briefly mention where and what you studied, if relevant.

WHAT YOU MAKE — This should include your chosen medium(s), the reasons for this choice and how you came to it. You can also discuss a little history of the medium(s), if applicable, as well as any benefits or limitations that come with them. Talk about your work in a literal sense and leave any interpretations for later. 'X makes large-scale abstract paintings using oil and tempera on canvas,' for example.

WHAT THE WORK IS ABOUT – Here you can talk about your intentions and inspirations, what you are trying to say or do in your work and what you may be responding to. It's better to focus on these than on interpretations – since the former you have control over, the latter you do not.

CAREER HIGHLIGHTS AND CURRENT/FUTURE PLANS – You can brag a little about where your work has been seen, but remember to keep the language purely objective. Include some of the most impressive shows you have been in, which collections hold your work and what exciting projects you have forthcoming. Much of this will already be covered in your CV, which is a separate document, so keep this section to no more than a couple of sentences. You can also add here a few short quotes about your work by respected art world figures if you have any, but again, don't feel the need to pad this section out too much.

When crafting your statement, you should always avoid platitudes, absolutes and exaggerations. Too often an artist's statement claims that the work can change the world, but this is rarely the case. Likewise, a good statement should not tell the reader what to see. Rather, explain why things are as they are and let readers come to their own conclusions. There is also a common compulsion to write texts of this kind in the most obscure and unintelligible language possible: what has come to be known as International Art Speak. This rarely helps to convey any salient information as the style and language often cause the reader to abandon the text before finishing it. Instead, a good statement should be clear, concise and informative. Phrases like 'this work forces the viewer to question the nature of their own reality' are a very clear sign that the artist is trying to over-intellectualize their work. Try not to focus too much on what you may have read in other artists' statements and avoid feeling like this document needs to sound clever. Also, try to avoid including claims that may not be true, just because you feel they may be what gallerists and curators want to hear. If your work doesn't have an ecological focus, for example, don't try to claim that it does primarily because that may be a very relevant topic at this particular moment.

Try not to give too much away. Instead, allow the audience to discover some things for themselves. Ultimately, your artist statement should explain enough about yourself and your work that readers feel like they understand you better after reading it, while still leaving space for their own interpretations. It is not your place (or your responsibility) to say what your work means, merely what it is, what inspired or informed it and why you made it. Think of your personal statement not as a thinly veiled scholarly review of your work, but as a roadmap with which the viewer can better navigate your work.

Whether to write your statement in the first or third person is a perennial question upon which there seems to be no real consensus. Using the first person ('I am ...') can seem too personal and at times unprofessional, whereas using the third person ('The artist is ...') can seem pretentious. Both can be used effectively, and both can be done badly. One of the main reasons for writing in the third person is that this makes it easier for galleries and publications to pull from – the easier you can make this task, the better. When making the decision, try to imagine who will be reading this text and why. Also think about what sounds most natural, and what version of yourself you would like to convey. If you find it hard to write in the third person you can always write it in the first person and then edit it into the third person once the whole text has been written.

Think about ways in which you can explain what it is you do and why, without feeling as if you need to emulate statements you may have read in the past.

If you are struggling to write your artist statement it would be a good idea to find some written by your contemporaries. Go to the website of a gallery you admire and see how the statements have been written for the artists they represent. This will help you develop a language that you can apply to your own work, but remember, make it personal to you and your work, without copying too closely the statements written by others. Use this as a place where you can show off your ability to discuss art and really express your personality at the same time.

On Being an Artist and a Parent

DR CHARLEY PETERS

Dr Charley Peters is an artist working in painting and public art, making works that engage with the expanded contexts of painting in the digital age. She has a PhD in fine art theory and practice and is Head of Graduate School at City & Guilds of London Art School.

Being an artist is the best job in the world, one that most of us are grateful to be doing and can't live without. It's a lifelong journey filled with inspiration, wonder, intellectual stimulation and creative energy – there is nothing else like it.

But what happens when you become a parent, and the career path that you were on takes a detour? Is it really possible to do everything? Can you still be a 'proper' artist, achieving recognition and hitting all your creative goals while simultaneously raising children? Well, yes, you can ... but maybe not in the same way as if you were just looking after yourself. This is okay. Both your career as an artist and your life as a whole are your own journeys to make, and you can go in all the unconventional directions that you need to in order to reach that destination. The path you are on as an artist parent might not be the same as it is for other artists, but over time you will find the means to navigate it in your own unique way. You will get there – or somewhere else equally exciting – and often the diversions along the way end up being the best parts of the adventure.

There are many variables to a life as an artist parent: our career goals, our financial circumstances and our children's needs are all different, and we deal with the day-to-day experiences of managing a creative career and a family differently. It's important for us to learn how to make things work on our own terms and to do our best to filter out the things that make doing everything even more difficult than it already is. Through the years I have learned many important things that have enhanced my experiences of both my career as an artist and my role as a parent, and, maybe more importantly, my understanding of myself.

I've been a parent for the past sixteen years, and a single parent for most of that time. It's taken me until my child is almost an adult to talk honestly about this and in most cases to even mention that I'm a parent in any professional context at all. I've spent most of my child's life assuming that people won't think that I'm a serious artist if they know that my focus and attention often have to be somewhere other than the studio, and feeling embarrassed to say that I couldn't go to private views, apply for residencies, attend meetings that were scheduled at the same time as the school run or be at the studio 24/7 to host the visits for those career-changing art-world connections that everyone told me I should be doing. I feel sad about this now, and wish I'd been more proud that I was raising a child alone at the same time that I was trying to paint, chase commissions, teach at a university, work as a freelance art writer and share my successes on social media with the deliberate strategy of making it all look easy. It is true that artists with children have been sidelined, excluded or under-represented in the conventional structure of the art world. There are, however, some positive things that we can do to start to reframe our experiences of artist parenthood in a way that allows us to take some power back.

Beliefs can be empowering motivators that help us to make good decisions and reach our goals, but when they are outdated or overly rigid, they can also be limiting, negative and – quite frankly – destructive. However, what is often hard about being a parent and an artist are those beliefs that are based on other people's opinions about how we should be living our lives. There isn't only one way to be *either* a parent or an artist – our experiences are meant to be a reflection of us as individuals. One of the most well-known quotes about creativity and parenthood is by the British writer Cyril Connolly: 'There is no more sombre enemy of good art than the pram in the hall.' He wrote this in 1938. Even if it was a valid thought then, it is nothing but judgemental and entitled today. Unfortunately, somehow Connolly's ghost is still haunting us. It's the voice in our heads that convinces us that once we have children we'll be viewed as being too distracted from the rigour of the studio, our artistic brains soiled by the reality of caring for something other than our own artwork. But Connolly's message that if you have children then you'll be creatively ruined forever has no basis in reality, and in fact our experiences can be the complete opposite of this. I realize now that I have only made the work I do *because* I had a child. When they were a baby I started to see the world as if for the first time, being reminded that everything around us can be inspiring and interesting, and ours to discover if we are receptive to it. It made me realize that life was happening now, and that now was all that mattered. I'll always be very grateful for this, and I hope that other artists who are parents make a similar realization.

There are some very real difficulties being an artist and a parent, and there's no definitive way of fixing these other than finding strategies to work around them in a way that is right for you. Our time often has non-negotiable constraints on it in ways that impact our productivity and ability to focus. We have to learn to be mentally agile and to use whatever time we have to make progress. We don't always need to be physically doing things in order to be working. Artists do a lot of work in our minds too, moving through ideas and solving creative problems without 'making' anything at all. It's hard not to think that you're missing out on a great career by having a child, but really that's just fear talking. The art world is a competitive place: there are not enough galleries, collectors or access to funding to offer opportunities for all the great artists working today, whether they are parents or not.

These days there is much more awareness of these inequalities, and there are positive changes being made by some institutions already. Unfortunately, this is a slow process and in the meantime we still have to carry on doing our thing and being the best that we can be in whatever ways we can. If you can't network and build meaningful relationships with galleries, curators and commissioners in person then you can find ways to reach people online by developing a strategy for using social media: organizing online meetings and sending newsletters to share with them what you are working on. It's important to connect with other artists too, as we are our own most supportive community and the best source of opportunities. Taking responsibility for making sure that others see your work even when you feel pulled in other directions is important. You have the power to make an impact every time you share your work with others. Make it a habit to focus on what you have achieved and not what you haven't. And be proud of yourself, always.

We often focus on how being a parent affects our experiences of being an artist, but I think we should also look at things the other way around. I'd like to think that we are good parents *because* we are artists. Artists are naturally curious, unconventional, thoughtful and resilient – and these are *great* traits for a parent to have. Through our experience of being an artist we develop high-level skills in problem solving, creative thinking and endurance. Often without realizing, we are transferring new knowledge and experiences from the studio to the home and back again, our development as both artist and parent uniting in a way that ultimately gives us holistic strength as a person. For me, one of the best things that being an artist parent gave me was the potential to inspire my child by designing a life that is creative, enriching and atypical. Once we learn to do things in our own unique way in order to keep everything afloat, we are also showing by example that our children are free to live their lives the way that they want (or need to) when they are adults.

Having a child helped me, probably for the first time in my life, to be my best. How I have framed the goal of being the best artist and parent has evolved over time through a process of honest and sometimes painful reflection. Instead of trying to be *the* best, I started to focus on being *my* best. Through this shift in focus I realized that much of what I saw as 'success' was based on other people's ideals, many of which referenced twentieth-century models of being an artist in a gallery system that does still exist, but is now not the only (or even most interesting) way of being an artist. Everyone's model of success, and their timeline to achieve it, are different. As artist parents we might achieve our goals later because we have other things to focus on besides our work, but that's okay because we'll reach them at a point when we are more experienced and informed, and have had time to appreciate the significance of them.

Difference is good, and creative people are excellent at doing things differently.

Open Calls

Open calls can be a great way to have your work seen, to exhibit in places that would otherwise be difficult and to submit your work to galleries that don't otherwise accept submissions. There are many different types of open call out there, and it can sometimes be hard to know which opportunity is a worthwhile use of your time and which isn't.

If an open call is free to enter, then all you risk losing by doing so is the time you spent filling out the application. If you have time, there's no harm in trying, as the ones you are accepted for will likely make up for those you aren't. Also, once you have a well-constructed artist statement and CV, the time taken to apply to open calls will decrease as you won't have to start from scratch each time. Writing proposals is a common practice for many artists, and the experience you gain in applying for open calls will be beneficial even if you aren't accepted into the exhibition itself.

If you do decide to enter, it's important to ensure that you completely fulfil the requirements set out by the hosting institution or gallery. For example, if there is a theme, your work should fit it and not seem out of place in the event you are selected (although it's highly unlikely you would be). These guidelines exist for a reason, and all you will achieve by ignoring them is to annoy the selection committee and ensure that they don't select you for inclusion. If you don't have any work that fits the theme and you have time to make something new that will, then you can always take the time to make it. If you do decide to do this, though, it should be work you would be able and happy to use in the future for something else should the opportunity arise.

The benefits of being accepted can make the admin of applying worth it. Winning something (or being short-listed) looks great on your CV. As well as this, some of the artists involved will be bound for great success in the near future, and being associated with them as a fellow winner of an open call places you in the same bracket. Esteem by association is still esteem.

Sharing wall space with excellent artworks in a prestigious and professional-looking gallery can also take your CV, website and social media to the next level. Artwork often looks great in a studio, but there is no replacement for the pristine white walls and excellent lighting of a gallery to make your work look as good as it possibly can. The documentation of the exhibition is usually a responsibility of the gallery, and so another added benefit is that you'll get some excellent photos to use to show how professional and alluring your work can be.

When there *is* an entry fee to submit, it is important to do a cost–benefit analysis. If the gallery is very prestigious or will attract many visitors, it could perhaps be worth it. It is also a good way to have your work seen by the selection panel, who might single you out in future for something else if they liked your work. Paying an entry fee is perhaps more reasonable when the space you will be exhibiting in is a prestigious gallery in a prime location where many people will see your work. These open calls often offer prizes in the form of cash, residencies or mentoring that can also make them worthwhile. When this same fee is charged by smaller galleries, and especially when there are no other prizes besides being included in the exhibition, it seems a lot less reasonable.

Aside from an entry fee, you should also consider the other costs involved should you be selected. These may include handling such as packing, shipping and insuring your work, but you should never be charged for hanging or promotion. If you decide to attend the opening, you may also need to factor in transport and accommodation, as these are unlikely to be paid for you. The works may need to be delivered and collected on a specific day, too, so this is likely to complicate things for you slightly, and possibly increase the cost of transportation.

Sadly, some organizations seem to use the entry fee from their open call to finance other, less successful elements of their programme. That's not to say that all pay-to-enter open calls do this, for there can be a lot of admin that goes into organizing one, and the entry fee can go some way to recouping these costs. The entry fee is also a useful way for galleries to limit the size of the application pool, as only artists who are serious about their practice are likely to apply if there is a fee involved. It's important to judge every opportunity on its merits. Not every free-to-enter open call is great, and not every open call with an entry fee is bad.

There are some open calls out there that advertise themselves as being free to enter, but then charge a 'hanging fee' or similar for those artists who are selected for inclusion in the exhibition (or publication, as this happens with those too). Open calls like this are usually worth avoiding, as this is most often a tactic of 'vanity galleries' and only serves to exploit the excitement that early-career artists may feel when they hear that they have been successful in their application. It is likely that the vast majority of applicants (if not all of them) have been 'successful', and the gallery is willing to show any artist who will pay the fee.

On the whole, try to think about what each open call can actually offer you (instead of what they might claim to be offering), and base your decisions upon this. If you think carefully about which to enter and which to avoid, you can save yourself not only the cost of the entrance but also the time spent on the application. It is unlikely you will be accepted for everything you apply for, but this is just a part of what it means to be an artist. No unsuccessful application represents a personal failure, as there are so many factors at play that determine who is selected and who isn't, but if you spend time carefully researching any open calls you come across and then make the best applications you can possibly make, you are giving yourself the best chances of success.

Payment or Exposure?

Early on in your career, you might be offered some opportunities that are unpaid. You may be asked to install some work in a cafe or bar, create some work that will be used to advertise or illustrate something, or paint a mural.

If a potential company or client can clearly afford to pay you and is just choosing not to, then the arrangement is likely exploitative and should be avoided. However, if they are in a similar position to you and the relationship seems as if it will be more of a collaborative effort than a transaction heavily weighted in their favour, you may decide that it is worthwhile.

You'll often be told that you shouldn't work for free, usually by people who have done so in the past but can afford not to now, and this advice can harm your career if you take it too literally. Like most creative careers, being an artist usually begins as a passion or hobby, and in the early days, you'll be content to do it purely for enjoyment. Unlike most hobbies, though, it can eventually become a career if approached correctly.

While we would recommend getting paid wherever possible, sometimes there are more valuable rewards to be had. There are many possible benefits to this type of collaboration, so each opportunity should be considered carefully before you decide whether to agree to do it. Connections to like-minded individuals or artists at a similar place in their careers are incredibly important for an early-career artist, and any opportunity to make more of these will be helpful. If you do agree to work for free, it's possible that the connections you make and the experience you gain will benefit your career in the long run. There are many insights that can be gained when we approach collaborative projects with an open mind, even if this is just more knowledge about what you do and don't want to take part in.

While you shouldn't really be giving your work away for free in the hope that the receiver will help you later down the line, working alongside others towards a shared goal can be a great experience that brings you closer together. It takes time to learn how to operate in the art world, and sometimes the collaborative environment is a good place to test things out, without the pressure and stress that paid opportunities will bring.

Selling Your Work

If you are selling your own work, there are a few things you should consider doing to make this process run smoothly. For example, selling in a high volume can be good for some things (money helps you pay the bills) and harmful for others (with more sales, scarcity diminishes). Below we've listed some of the most common topics that we get asked about in the hope that this will help you make informed decisions about your own sales if and when they occur. It should also be said that the below applies mainly to artists seeking representation in the 'fine art' area of the art world, who are either working with galleries already or hope to in the future.

PRICING

Knowing how to price your work can be difficult. The time spent working, the materials and your own CV need to be considered when making these decisions. The most efficient way to do this is to look at the prices of comparable works by artists at a similar level to you (and be honest about who these individuals are), and use them as a starting point. Determine who these contemporaries are by style and medium of work, where they are exhibiting or selling, and how many shows they have had. It is easy to make these pricing decisions poorly at an early stage in your career and then have to correct them later, so you should consider this carefully early on. While it is true that some artists set their prices high early on and sell well, this usually isn't sustainable in the long term. Collectors will spend a long time researching you before buying your work, and they will see if the price is over-inflated based on where you are in your career.

Over-pricing might dissuade potential sales, but under-pricing can be damaging in a different way. At the beginning of your career, it's always a good idea to price your art on the lower end so that there is room to grow. However, it can be tempting to sell works at a lower price point regularly, rather than trying to sell expensive works every now and then. Selling smaller and more affordable works is fine, but selling too many can erode the demand for your larger works, too.

One common (but problematic) way of determining the price is to measure the work, multiplying its height by its width to get the area, before multiplying this number by some predetermined figure to determine the price. The problem with this method is that it can make your prices seem inconsistent, even if they aren't. Instead, we should price a little more intuitively, so as to not dissuade any sales. Works of a similar size should be a similar price, but don't stick rigidly to a mathematical formula when it is emotions that drive not only the creation of the work, but also the decisions a buyer will be making when considering whether to purchase.

It is always best for the price to be a nice round number, making it as clear and easy to understand as possible. £500 is a much nicer price than £546.33, for example, and those extra two digits on the end (despite coming after a decimal point and not a comma) make the figure *seem* a lot larger than it is. By rounding this figure down to £500 or up to £550 you avoid any messy mathematical calculations the potential buyer might be doing in their head and allow them to focus entirely on their feelings towards the work itself. This is invaluable, and far trumps the £50 or so you may lose.

GALLERY SALES VS DIRECT SALES

If you're signed to a gallery that has the exclusive right to show and sell your work, you shouldn't be selling works directly to buyers yourself at the same time. This will most likely be stated explicitly in the contract you signed with the gallery anyway, but you should ensure that you know what is and isn't agreed upon before you sign it. If a gallery has the exclusive right to sell your work, it will probably be thinking more long-term than you might be with each sale. For example, the gallerist may want to be selective over who they sell to (to place works in prestigious collections, for example) or limit the amount of available work to sustain the demand.

If you aren't signed to a gallery but do sometimes exhibit with them, you should keep your pricing the same whether the work is sold directly from you, or through a gallery. If a gallery finds out that you are undercutting it, it will have less incentive to work with you, as galleries know that collectors will go directly to you if the prices are cheaper. If you have a 'studio price' and a 'gallery price', it will look like your prices jump around all over the place, and individuals (including collectors and galleries) will notice. If someone buys a work from your studio and then sees similar works for a much higher price elsewhere, it will look like you've artificially inflated your prices. Meanwhile, if someone sees the gallery price first and then receives a quote from your studio, it will look like you've dropped your prices overnight. These are all bad signs to be putting out there.

You are able to sell works directly from your studio if you are showing with galleries but aren't formally signed with them, but this should be done carefully. You should still try to avoid upsetting that gallery–artist relationship, so don't advertise this option too publicly while you have exhibitions open, and don't start selling very similar works to those currently in a show.

Here's a big thing to avoid: some artists will receive enquiries about a work that is under consignment with a gallery and choose to not mention this to the gallery, ask for that work back, and then sell it themselves once they have received it. It is always best to pass these enquiries on to the gallery as the buyer will probably have sent it the same enquiry that they sent you, and may tag the gallery in posts about the work once they have received it, too. Your plan will then be clear to all involved, and it makes you look underhand. These galleries will avoid working with you in future. (See 'What Does a Consignment Agreement Look Like?', p. 165, for further information regarding this.)

DISCOUNTS

A 10 per cent discount is pretty much the industry standard. Sometimes 15 per cent is allowed and, in special circumstances, 20 per cent. These will never be advertised, and a gallery may choose to give a 10 per cent discount without even mentioning it to you, instead choosing to absorb the loss from its own share of the profits. If a small discount can help secure a sale, most will give it. The larger discounts are only really given when a buyer is taking multiple works, has bought a lot in the past or is a particularly well-known or influential collector. Your gallery will likely speak to you about any larger discounts before agreeing, and may ask you to share the costs. This is nothing to be afraid of as long as they don't breach the 20 per cent mark. Some artists are more flexible than others with these requests; erring on the side of flexibility here is usually a good approach. (Public discounts and promotions are a different beast entirely, and are explained more fully below.)

ONLINE SHOPS

Having work listed online with clear pricing and an easy-to-use user experience can increase your sales overall. However, if you are planning to exhibit in galleries, having too much work visibly listed for sale on your own website can send the wrong message. It can be a negative thing for some of the reasons listed above, and so should be done sparingly and discreetly. It is also a bad thing to have work remaining visibly unsold online for too long, so if you do go down this route, it is usually best to limit the timeframe for this kind of thing. If works remain unsold for a long period of time this can signal a lack of demand, which sometimes puts people off. Prints and editioned works are slightly different, and can remain listed for longer without the negative connotations associated with original works.

TAX

The tax arrangement for each country will be different and so we can't be too specific here. However, regardless of where you are in the world (with very few exceptions), once you have earned over a certain amount in the tax year you will be liable to pay tax on your earnings. If, like many artists, you have a day job aside from your artistic practice, it may be that the tax rate is higher on what is deemed your 'second' job. If this is the case, speak to a tax advisor about the best way to handle this, as it is sometimes beneficial to have your artistic practice as your 'first job' even if it earns less income, as the expenses you can claim on your artistic practice can save you some tax expenditure if recorded. (See 'Filing Your Taxes', p. 187, for more on this.)

VAT (Value Added Tax) is another thing you may have to charge on each work, but again this will differ from country to country. Certain items attract different VAT rates, and some may be exempt from VAT entirely (such as, at the time of writing, books in the UK), so make sure you research this, too. You may be able to claim back any VAT you have paid, so it is worthwhile knowing what your individual position is on this as early as possible. VAT may only be applicable once you have made over a certain amount of sales, and so again we would recommend speaking to a tax advisor to ensure you have all of this worked out in time for your tax return.

SALES OR PROMOTIONS

These can drastically improve your likelihood of selling, but should generally be avoided if your aim is to inhabit the more 'fine art' area of the art world. Art is something that many people buy for investment reasons, and even if you are primarily selling to people who are buying purely because they like it, its speculative potential will still be somewhere in their minds. Sales, discount codes and promotions make the work look cheap at best, and your standard prices look too expensive at worst. They may help you sell a few in the short term, but could harm your more long-term prospects.

In general, selling your work should be a pleasant, mutually beneficial agreement between two parties who both believe that they are the ones getting the best deal. It is a beautiful thing to have something you have made go out into the world and adorn the walls of someone's home, but sometimes the transactional element of the sale of an artwork can diminish that beauty. Hopefully, in this short chapter we have made some of the elements of this less obscure so that your future sales will be easier and smoother to handle.

Controlling Your Output

If you are selling original artworks, it is not always a good idea to sell as much as you possibly can. This is especially the case for fine artists, who will need to be more selective than those who sell more affordable works or reproductions. For example, if you are lucky enough to start showing in commercial galleries, they may want to limit your output to create or nurture a demand for your work. A key part of demand is scarcity, so limiting availability can encourage collectors to buy quickly for fear of missing out.

This can sound counterintuitive, because many sales and shows early on in your career can help to establish you as a part of the art world, and as someone worth investing in.

However, as your career progresses, and your prices start creeping higher (more on that in a minute), it is important to not over-produce in an attempt to cater for increasing demand. If you find yourself showing or selling work that you aren't entirely happy with, this may be a sign that you are over-producing. Remember, a huge part of having great work lies in employing some strict quality control, and not exhibiting work that isn't a good representation of you or your practice. It is often better for your career in the long run to only show what you feel is your best work, even if this means you ultimately sell a little less.

It is also important to pay attention to the message you are putting out there by over-producing. If you are constantly churning out works and making them available for sale, you are signalling to any potential buyer that they don't need to rush: they can take their time, and more work will be available soon. This discourages people from buying, and if your aim is to exhibit with an established commercial gallery, you should try to avoid it. None of this means that you should make less work, however, just that as sales increase it will become more and more important to limit what gets seen and sold. One action that galleries will take in this regard is to only show the number of works they think they can sell. This may sound counter-intuitive to begin with, but consider these two scenarios. If a gallery is exhibiting fifty paintings and sells ten, they have sold one-fifth of what is available. However, if the show only includes ten paintings, then it is a sell-out. This sounds incredibly impressive and is likely to increase the likelihood of sales in later shows, as the buyers who considered buying last time but didn't, won't want to miss out again.

Something else to be careful with is the rate at which you raise your prices. Most early-career artists either find themselves afraid to raise their prices at all, or they do so far too quickly. Pricing your work is a hard thing to get right and is something that many artists agonize over. Starting with low prices can feel as if you do not value your work, so many emerging artists feel the need to set their prices high to show that they do. Actually, though, it is far better to allow for growth by starting on the lower end of the scale because then your work will begin to make its way into people's homes and out of your workspace, instead of you having to show and store the same works over and over again because they are so expensive. The transition from art being a hobby to it being a career is a gradual one and will involve some investment from you before the latter becomes a possibility. If you try to sell your work for higher-than-reasonable prices at a very early stage in your career, you are likely going to make less over-all income from that work than if you priced it more rea-sonably. Even if you aren't making enough to cover the materials, your time and all your other expenses, it is still likely to be more profitable than most hobbies already. With this approach, over time sales will hopefully increase, and you will be able to cover more and more of your ex-penses by selling work.

Starting off with high prices may be tempting and can seem to give your work a certain respectability. However, collectors will always do their research before they part with large sums of money, and over-priced works will always be identifiable. Raising your prices too fast can have a negative impact, too, as you may have to drop them just as quickly if the sales aren't there to support the price point, and this looks bad for obvious reasons.

Sales are nice, but until you are surviving entirely off your artwork, they shouldn't be the only quantifier by which you measure your own success. If you want to build a lasting demand for your work, you should not rush into selling as much as possible, as quickly as possible. Remember that purchasing decisions are made based on emotional responses before logical ones and that how you conduct your career, what you make available and how often, and how you set your prices can all have large and potentially harmful implications if not handled carefully.

Being Represented

Finding a gallery that will represent you is another of those steps that early-career artists feel is necessary to become a 'proper artist'. It is true that there are some great benefits to being represented, but there are also some limitations on what you are and aren't able to do. Here we've tried to elucidate some of what it means to be represented and to help you decide whether or not it is something you want to pursue. The particulars of these agreements will differ from gallery to gallery, so the below is only intended to outline what an agreement is for.

WHAT IS REPRESENTATION?

Representation is essentially an agreement between the artist and the gallery (sometimes officially and in writing) stating each party's responsibilities in relation to the other. They are intended to be mutually beneficial, and create a closer connection between the artist and gallery than either may have with others who aren't included in a similar arrangement. If a gallery signs an artist to its roster, it is often committing to host a set amount of shows (both group and solo) featuring the signed artist each year, either in the gallery or at art fairs. Galleries will usually test out an artist in group shows to see if the relationship feels like a good fit and to see if their collector base seems interested in the work, so don't expect a representation offer immediately once you are invited to exhibit with a gallery.

WHY GALLERIES SIGN ARTISTS

When a gallery signs an artist it is able to have a closer input into what happens to that artist's works, often with first refusal over including them in shows, and a say in what other galleries the artist works with. All of these decisions are made in good faith with the artist's continued success in mind, because success for one naturally leads to success for the other. The gallery is committing to invest time, resources and energy into developing the artist in the hope that this growing success benefits both parties. When an artist is signed by one gallery they may not be able to work with all of the other galleries that would like to include them in shows. Galleries want the artist's work to sell, but they also want there to be room for growth.

PRIMARY REPRESENTATION

It is possible to be signed by many galleries at once (for example, you may have a London gallery and a New York gallery), all of whom represent your interests in their respective city or country. Many artists who are signed to multiple galleries will have 'primary representation' with one of them, usually in their home city, who has the largest stake in the artist's career. This gallery has the most invested and the largest say on what the artist is and isn't involved in. When you show with other galleries, your primary representative may take a small percentage of the sales that occur, and may want to be involved in any decision-making. (Often their take is around 10 per cent, which comes out of the other gallery's share, which is reduced to 40 per cent; the remaining 50 per cent will go to the artist – but these numbers may vary). Your primary representative will also help to promote these shows with other galleries, as your success is something they have a vested interest in.

SOME OF THE BENEFITS

The greatest benefit of signing with a gallery is the advice and guidance you will receive from the gallery that has your best interests at heart. It is in its interest to help you grow and develop your career, and so you can hopefully be more trusting of this advice than you might be about advice received from others. Many gallerists, dealers and collectors are only interested in cashing in and cashing out, so the longevity of the artist's career isn't a concern for them, and their actions can sometimes harm your career in the long run. This isn't the case for a gallery that officially represents you, however, as they are in it for the long run too.

Another benefit is that they will often take care of a lot of the admin for you. If it is them selling your work, they will also be responsible for packing, shipping, insuring and invoicing. They will often photograph your works and promote them extensively to their followers and collectors' lists. Being included on the list of represented artists by a respected gallery gives you some of that respectability, and validates your work as it has their backing.

Being signed to a gallery means accepting that it now has some say over your career. This can feel limiting and frustrating if the gallerist wants to control your output or the other shows that you take part in, and you may not always agree about what is best for your career. These issues can often be talked through, but an agreement may not always be reached and in these instances whatever is in the official contract will have to be deferred to.

These days it is less essential to be signed to a gallery early on in your career than it once was, and now galleries usually wait until you have proven your ability to succeed on your own before they will consider signing you. Some artists do incredibly well having never signed to a gallery, while some others' careers skyrocket when they are picked up by the right gallery.

It can be tempting to rush into a representation agreement with a gallery as it can feel like this makes your position as a 'proper artist' more legitimate, but remember these agreements often come with written contracts that are hard to get out of. If you do decide to sign with a gallery make sure that you do your research into its reputation, perhaps speaking to other artists who are represented by it (and perhaps most usefully some who once were, but are no longer) so that you can ensure that it is the right decision for you, and it is happening at the right time.

What Does a Consignment Agreement Look Like?

Not all galleries work with official consignment agreements, preferring instead to work on trust and mutual respect. It is often the more commercial galleries who will insist on one, but these documents are nothing to be feared, and when understood they can give both parties some reassurance that they are working in each other's best interests.

Consignment is essentially a loan of your work, with the agreement that the gallery is able to sell it on your behalf. It does not mean that they buy the work from you, or that they are guaranteeing a sale in any way, and signing a consignment agreement does not mean that the gallery legally owns the work. Below is a short list of what you can expect to find if you are ever asked to sign one, or if you ever feel the need to request one from a gallery.

THE NAMES OF BOTH PARTIES, THEIR CONTACT DETAILS, THE DATE This is fairly self-explanatory. It may include your name at the start and thereafter refer to you as 'the artist' or 'the consigner', but this will be made clear and isn't anything to worry about.

WHAT IS BEING CONSIGNED The titles, dimensions, medium, year of creation, edition number (if applicable) and price. These will probably already have been agreed on ahead of time. The price should be given, including the gallery commission, which is outlined below. It should also be listed in the currency in which the work will be sold. If the gallery is in the US, for example, they will be selling the work in dollars and this should be made clear in the pricing you discuss with them, as the exchange rate at the date of consignment may be vastly different from when the work sells.

GALLERY COMMISSION How much the gallery takes, as a percentage of each sale. This is usually 50 per cent, sometimes lower, but it should never be higher. Some galleries include charges such as VAT or framing into the price of the work (by increasing it) so as to not put off buyers with additional fees on top of the sale price. In these instances, their commission may seem larger than 50 per cent to account for these additional charges. (This type of agreement definitely isn't common, but it is the preferred way of working for some galleries.) For those who do find themselves working with a gallery that prefers this type of arrangement: VAT isn't payable in all countries and so the gallery should only take that higher percentage when VAT is applicable, and not in all cases.

DISCOUNT PERCENTAGE Discounts are common, and nothing to be afraid of. Ten per cent is fairly standard and most buyers who ask for it will get it. The consignment agreement will likely only include the fact that the standard discount is allowed, and that anything larger will be discussed by both parties.

SHIPPING AND INSURANCE RESPONSIBILITIES

Insurance is usually handled by the gallery while it is in possession of the work. Either shipping the work is covered both ways by the gallery, or you will have to get the work to them and they will return it if unsold. Sometimes galleries will insist that the artist covers shipping both ways, but never should it be the responsibility of the artist to get the work from the gallery to the buyer. Larger and more established galleries will cover shipping both ways, but for galleries working with early-career artists it's often too expensive and too much of a risk to pay for all the shipping without any guarantee of sales, and so many won't.

CONSIGNMENT DURATION AND EXCLUSIVITY

The gallery will always want exclusive rights to promote and sell the works that it holds, for the duration of the show (and up to one year afterwards). This can lead to your works sitting in the gallery's storage for a long time after the show, but as sales can take a while to be finalized and can trickle in slowly, long after the show, this isn't anything to worry about. Any work that is available with one gallery shouldn't be offered to another gallery or for sale privately until the consignment period is up. In rare cases, it may be possible to negotiate a loan if both galleries are comfortable with it, but they will likely each prefer exclusive works.

TERMINATION This details the requirements should either party wish to terminate the agreement. It could include specific notice periods that both parties must adhere to.

PAYMENT DATE This might be longer than you would imagine, for a multitude of reasons. Galleries often reserve works for a short time to give the potential buyer some time to decide. They will then need to wait until the show is over, arrange shipping quotes and pass these on to the buyer (who may then take a while to pay). Shipping work takes time, especially if overseas, and delays at the border are fairly common with objects of high value. The buyer will often pay 50 per cent upfront and the balance once the artwork arrives, and some bank transactions can take a while to clear, especially international transfers. To allow for all of this, and other unforeseen delays, consignment agreements will often err on the side of caution and go for the maximum duration between completion and payment to the artist. Thirty days is common, but some go as far as ninety. (Note that this is thirty days after the payment from the buyer has been transferred, and not from the date the sale was agreed.)

PROMOTIONAL RESPONSIBILITIES It may be that galleries use the consignment agreement to ensure that both parties are doing their best to promote the show/work, but is rarely any more specific than this.

OTHER ALLOWANCES This section may or may not be present, but if it is it will likely deal with matters such as image usage, detailing whether or not the gallery can reproduce images of the work for promotional purposes or to create prints or other kinds of merchandise.

SIGNATURES OF BOTH PARTIES As you would expect.

Operating Outside the Traditional Gallery Model

As an artist, it can be disheartening to make work that you believe in but that attracts limited to no interest from commercial galleries. Some artists may decide not to wait for galleries to seek them out and instead operate entirely outside this arena. There are many things you can do to facilitate this if you pursue that option, and these activities will often actually *increase* your visibility to those galleries you wish to attract.

The goal for many of these artists is to reach a point where they are able to sell works independently, without needing the backing of an established gallery to give that work validation. If you have the contacts for this, or believe you can obtain them, there is no reason not to pursue this. Artists often begin by selling smaller and more affordable works to friends and family, and this group of potential buyers usually grows over time. Don't jeopardize personal relationships by forcing discussions that involve money, though. It is often best to make it clear that you are approachable and let these people come to you if they want to buy something. Likewise, if you have a sale in progress with anyone from this group and it seems to lose steam before it's completed, it is best to let the buyer back out without any coercion or implied inconvenience. They want to support you, but pushing too hard will only make them reluctant to approach you in future.

To enlarge this circle of potential buyers, one option is to involve yourself in craft fairs or other events that bring different creatives together under one roof. This may become the main way your work is seen publicly and can help with exposure to people outside your own circles. Engaging with other creatives who are showing and selling their work at fairs can also be a useful way to share experience, facilities or opportunities. Throughout your career, you will find that it's other artists who provide the firmest network of support. So, it is them that you should be trying to get to know, rather than gallerists, curators, critics or collectors. Where artists go, others will follow.

Prints and reproductions are other great ways to generate an income from your work, and it is easier than ever to make these yourself. Many online platforms now offer print-on-demand services, where you can upload an image that is then printed and shipped directly without you having to invest in a large edition of printed items in advance. Many artists release prints on paper, as well as T-shirts, tote bags, greeting cards and almost anything else you can imagine. As reproductions, the price of these will always be lower than your original work, but it is much easier to sell them at a higher volume and with less effort, alongside your original work.

A note of caution should probably be made on this point: be careful not to devalue your original work by releasing cheap and unprofessional reproductions of it. Everything should make sense with your practice and be as well thought out as the work itself. It is rarely the case that cheap mass-produced 'merchandise' will help further your career, but well-thought-out, tasteful reproductions need not be avoided. For fine artists, limited-edition artisanal prints (such as hand-pulled screenprints) are always a much better option than digital prints.

Pay-to-exhibit galleries are another potential avenue to explore, but as we discuss them in greater detail elsewhere in this book, we won't go over them again here. If you are happy to do all the promotion, invigilation and sales yourself then these can sometimes be a worthwhile option. However, a lot of the time these places seem to overpromise and under-deliver. Hired spaces are much more valuable than pay-to-exhibit galleries as they are free from some of the more negative connotations associated with such spaces. (See 'Starting Something Yourself', p. 97, for more details.)

Cafes and bars often commission artists to put on small exhibitions or paint inside their spaces, and these can be a great way to increase your visibility. If it's a commission then you should always be paid, but if it's an exhibition of artworks that you can either sell or take home with you afterwards, being paid is highly unlikely. Sometimes the venue will allow a small opening event, with either free or paid refreshments, and these are a great way to show your work and invite people to come and see it. There is also the added benefit of customers who are in the space seeing your work, as you never know how one of these chance encounters might impact your career down the line. Many successful artists began their careers this way, and if your list of previous exhibitions is a short one, you might choose to pursue something like this to help build your following.

Commissions are another excellent way to make money with your art, and as the sale is already guaranteed before the work is complete, it is often possible to do this without gallery involvement. Many artists are discovered via word of mouth, but there is no reason not to put yourself and your work out there as much as you can while you are waiting. When working on a commission it is usually a good idea to have the buyer pay some of the money in advance and the rest upon delivery of the work, but it should be as clear as possible what the arrangement is before any money is transferred or any work started. You may want to specify how many times you will make changes to the commission before extra charges are incurred, but at the beginning of your career it is often best not to frighten off any potential buyers with contracts that are too long and language that is incomprehensible without legal training.

Charities are always on the lookout for artists to collaborate with or to donate work to auctions and the like, and while this kind of relationship might not always get you paid, they can often lead to opportunities that do. If you can support yourself and have time to pursue these relationships early on in your career, they are more than worthwhile. Not only do you earn some good karma for helping worthy causes, but your work is also seen in often more prestigious areas than it might be otherwise.

Many successful artists started by doing some or all the things listed above. Operating in this way can also lead to gallery interest later on, as continually showing your work proves that you are driven. Choosing to avoid the traditional gallery model entirely is also fine, however, and many artists make a good living by working outside it.*

* These are all worthwhile pursuits if you aren't signed to a gallery and have total freedom in how and where your work is seen and sold. If you are signed to a gallery, it may want a say in what avenues you do and don't go down, and anything you do outside that relationship should be done carefully so as to not jeopardize it. If you are selling work independently this could lead to galleries feeling as if you aren't taking the relationship seriously or you are undermining their efforts. Essentially, if you sign a contract with a gallery, ensure that both parties are aware of what the responsibilities and expectations are on each side, and respect the arrangement that you have both agreed to.

Shipping Sold Works

If you are an artist who sells works privately – meaning anything sold not by someone acting on your behalf such as a gallery, shop or dealer – you will have to deal with shipping. Once a sale has been agreed, talk of shipping or delivery of the work will necessarily arise. If the collector wants to come and pick up the work themselves, this only makes your job easier. Similarly, they might want to organize their own shipping, which again is preferable to shipping the work yourself.

Unfortunately, it will often be up to you to arrange. If the collector is someone you know or doesn't live too far away, you may want to hand-deliver the work. This saves on expensive couriers or art handlers and allows you some more face-to-face time with the buyer, too.

The most likely scenario, though, is that the work will need to be shipped, and this can be annoyingly complex, even for people who have done it many times before.

Who pays for the shipping is something you and the collector will need to decide between yourselves. It is very common for the buyer to pay for all the packing, shipping and insurance costs, but some artists may decide to split this cost or cover it entirely if it helps secure the sale. Shipping costs added to the sale price are one of the most powerful disincentives for buyers, but many expect to have to pay shipping, so it is always best to approach this on a case-by-case basis. The most important thing is that no costs are 'hidden', so it should be clear if shipping is or isn't included in the price you quote the buyer.

Shipping artwork should always be handled carefully. The artwork should be packaged well and be able to withstand minor bumps and drops, as well as being left out in the rain for short amounts of time. It's always best to err on the side of caution here, as getting shipping or insurance companies to pay out in the event damage did occur is always an inconvenient hassle that no one needs (more on insurance later).

Any works on paper should be rolled if possible, and shipped inside a sturdy cardboard or plastic tube. The triangular prism-shaped shipping tubes are far less structurally sound than a regular cylindrical tube and are often more expensive. For added protection the work can be wrapped around one tube that is placed inside a larger one, but there should always be something like tissue paper to protect the delicate surface of the work. Balled-up bubble wrap or tissue paper should also be placed in both ends of the tube so that the edges of the work don't get damaged as the tube is turned either side up.

Framed works need to be packaged especially well as glass is particularly vulnerable to being broken and will almost certainly damage a paper work should it break. One way to mitigate this potential damage is to tape the entirety of the outside surface of the glass so that if it does break it will all stay together, but this should also be easy to remove and leave no residue. A box within a box is often a good way to protect framed works, with more bubble wrap, foam or polystyrene in between if possible. Some of these are more ecologically friendly than others, but it's easier now more than ever to find eco or recycled packaging materials. If this is possible for you then many buyers will also appreciate it.

Stretched canvases should be very well protected, as any drops or falls can tear the delicate canvas, which is difficult and expensive to repair. Any damage discovered upon arrival of the work is only going to upset the buyer and should be avoided at all costs.

The canvas should be crated if at all possible. For small works, it is possible to build crates yourself from designs found online, but larger, delicate or more valuable works will need to be crated professionally. Next, the piece itself should be separated from the edges of the crate with foam strips, but should be secured in place so it isn't moving around inside. (If using bubble wrap to protect a painting it is worth noting that if you wrap it bubble side in, the bubbles can adhere to the paint and leave marks when removed.)

The crate should be clearly labelled 'fragile' with markings or stickers, as well as arrows showing which way up the work should be transported, if this is important. A nice courtesy with any crated works is to label clearly which screws should be removed and in which order, as this will not only help the receiver in disassembling it, but also avoid any accidental damage they may inflict in trying to open it. Handles will also be appreciated for larger crates. A more cost-effective and simpler crate can be made out of rigid cardboard and bubble wrap, but the safety of the work should always be your top priority.

When shipping the work you will need to provide the haulage company with the dimensions, materials, value and weight of the shipment (this is another reason why you might want to measure and weigh each work as you complete it). You will also need to complete whatever customs declaration forms are necessary for your particular shipment. It is a good idea to get a self-adhesive plastic document wallet to affix to the package, as there may need to be multiple documents attached and they must be both visible and waterproof.

The shipment should be tracked at the very least, but it is always a good idea to insure the shipment for the full value of the work as well. Many shipping companies will have an option to include this on their site, but this isn't always the case (especially for larger or more expensive works), and so external insurance will need to be organized. Also, many commercial shipping companies' insurance policies don't cover 'artworks', so make sure you read the small print when ordering. There are many companies that exist for this specific purpose and insurance is easy to arrange online. If something is ever shipped uninsured it should always be at the buyer's request. If they understand and are willing to take the risk, they may ask for this as a way of keeping costs down. If they explicitly state that they are willing to shoulder the risk then on their head be it if anything goes wrong.

It's usually a good idea to shop around for both shipping and insurance, as some services are significantly more affordable than others. If the buyer is paying for shipping it is also a good idea to find a few quotes and allow them to choose which to go for, as they may opt for faster and more expensive or slower and cheaper shipping depending on their needs. Once the shipment is booked, all tracking info should be passed to the buyer, but you should also keep an eye on the progress of the shipment so you can assist with any customs delays.

Overall, shipping artworks is one of the least enjoyable and most stressful aspects of being an artist. One day you may reach a point in your career when a gallery will do all of this for you, but until that point, hopefully this short chapter will make that annoying process a little bit less stressful.

Cataloguing, Authenticity and Proof

Most artists hope to reach the level of esteem at which it becomes profitable for people to make counterfeits of their works. This is something that can damage the market for your work and your career overall if it isn't possible to prove what are and what aren't authentic pieces. This becomes more difficult to monitor as your career progresses, as earlier works are often forgotten entirely or misremembered, so start keeping track now.

The first thing you need to do is create a clear spreadsheet database of all your works with medium, title, size and other relevant details, and update this every time you make a create a new work or loan/sell an old one. It will help you to keep track of all the details, as well as being a clear indicator of what works are with which gallery. Following this you need to make a template certificate of authenticity (or COA) and give this to the buyer of each work. This is their proof that they possess a genuine artwork made by you and that they acquired it honourably, either directly or from someone (such as a gallery) acting on your behalf.

A Jackson Pollock painting was once proven authentic because it was analysed and found to contain a polar-bear hair. Photographs of his studio were then studied, and he was found to have had a polar-bearskin rug in some of the photos. If you create COAs for all your works and include the following details, you won't need to rely on accidental

bits of detritus to validate your artworks for you. COAs
also help you to keep track of what is where and will make
your life much easier in the long run.

CERTIFICATES OF AUTHENTICITY

Below is some of the information you may want to include
on your COAs.

YOUR NAME

ARTWORK TITLE Ensure that this is unique so as to
set the work apart from other works. If you prefer to
leave them untitled, consider giving them a catalogue
number to differentiate them.

ARTWORK DIMENSIONS Height, width and depth
is the standard for this. Use centimetres as standard,
but feel free to also include inches if you'd like.
Use 'dimensions variable' when the dimensions of
the work really are variable (for example, if it is site-
specific or moves) and not when the work is just a bit
hard to measure.

ARTWORK DATE The date it was created, not the date
it was sold.

MEDIUM List here everything used to make the work,
in as much detail as possible. This will help not only
to identify the work, but is also useful for future
conservation purposes.

THE POSITION OF THE ARTIST'S SIGNATURE Many people like to use the fancy term 'signed verso' to locate the signature on the back, but simply 'signed on the back' works just fine.

REPRODUCTION OF THE WORK A photograph of the work in the condition it was sold in. This will be helpful, if ever required to prove damage or alterations for resale or insurance purposes.

VISUAL DESCRIPTION Instead of using a photo, you may choose to describe the appearance of the work.

ITEM NUMBER It is a good idea to assign each work a unique number that is recorded both here and in your spreadsheet, so that it cannot be forged by someone without access to your personal database.

FIRST EXHIBITED/SOLD Not all COAs have this, but the more details you can include now, the easier you are making things for yourself later.

ARTIST'S SIGNATURE Sign it in ink. Not as big as John Hancock signed the Declaration of Independence, but make it visible.

GALLERY SIGNATURE/STAMP Again, this isn't 100 per cent necessary, but some artists choose to include it, especially if the COA is gallery-generated. Having a prestigious gallery visible is helpful for provenance but isn't essential.

DATE The date the COA was produced or signed.

Somewhere down the line in your career, you are going to need to keep track of all these details. Once this happens, you'll wish you had been doing it from the very beginning – so get started.

CATALOGUING

Alongside the COA you assign to each work, you should also have a spreadsheet in which you record them all. This makes it easier to keep track of everything and helps you to keep details consistent across the board. Below are some fields you will want to include here. Much of the information is the same as above so we won't repeat ourselves below.

TITLE The title of the work.

DIMENSIONS Height, width and depth.

YEAR When the work was made.

PRICE Including the price of the artwork helps you to be able to quote it quickly when asked, as well as ensuring that the prices of each work don't vary. Consider having the price in multiple currencies here if the buyer isn't in a country that uses the same currency as you, and be aware that exchange rates change over time.

EXHIBITION HISTORY Collectors will often ask for provenance, which is essentially a list of places the work has been exhibited in the past. Keeping track of this early on will make your life much easier in the future as you won't have to go trawling through old CVs to find this information when asked.

CATALOGUE NUMBER As explained above, this will help you to determine or locate artworks quickly. It can also be used to identify where something sits in your body of work, and if it is a legitimate work of yours.

INSPIRATIONS This isn't essential, but galleries or collectors may ask for further information about the piece, and if you don't note this down close to when the work was made you may forget and then have to conjure something up off the cuff, long after the work was completed.

SALES

One of the most valuable resources for an artist to possess is a record of all your previous buyers. As soon as someone enquires about purchasing something, you should take down their details and save them in a spreadsheet.

Make sure you compile the following information so as to better serve this potential returning customer in future.

BUYER'S NAME It is also a good idea to note down their preferred name so as not to cause any offence. Just because a name can be abbreviated doesn't mean that it always will be.

CONTACT INFORMATION Wherever possible try to record their personal email rather than any related to work or school, as if they leave then they will also lose access to that account and your messages won't get read.

LOCATION This is good information to have, as it can help with estimating shipping quotes or when deciding who to invite to each show.

THE WORK THEY WERE INTERESTED IN This will help you tailor your emails to them personally in future.

OTHER PERSONAL INFORMATION If you shared a connection over something you both liked, or you have something else in common, note it down so you can remember it.

OTHER WORKS/ARTISTS IN THE BUYER'S COLLECTION This can help you identify what they may or may not be interested in, so you can avoid contacting them about something you know they won't want to see.

If someone purchases something, they should be moved to a separate tab of the spreadsheet, and the following detail should be added.

THE WORK THEY PURCHASED This will help with any conservation or loan possibilities that may arise.

WHERE IT WAS PURCHASED

HOW MUCH THEY PAID This can give you an indication of what their budget may be in future, or which price bracket of works to show them should they enquire again.

ANY DISCOUNTS GIVEN Because they may expect it a second time if they buy from you again.

WHEN THE WORK WAS SHIPPED/DELIVERED

TRACKING INFORMATION

DELIVERY DATE

If you ever release a new series of works or have a show to announce, these contacts should hear about it before everyone else. It helps to foster a connection between yourself and them, and if they have bought your work before, they may do so again. It will also be useful further down the line if you ever need to identify the location of works, in case a gallery or museum ever wants to organize a retrospective of your work or arrange any loans.

Filing Your Taxes

Filing taxes really should be taught in art schools, but sadly isn't. The process is different depending on where you live in the world, and can seem overly complex and intimidating if you haven't done it before. Where possible, we have avoided using jargon and country-specific information, and so this section is necessarily non-specific and should be seen as advice on how to approach filing a tax return, rather than guidance on the exact details of the process. It is always important to double-check everything long before your accounts are due.

In our experience, registering and filing a tax return can be tricky, but there are professionals out there whose job it is to help you. The tax office in your country should be your first port of call, and it is in their best interest to make matters as clear and informative as possible. We would recommend giving them a call with any issues or questions you may have as soon as possible, just to get over the fear of completing your return in the first place.

REGISTERING AS A BUSINESS OR AS SELF-EMPLOYED

There are benefits to both, but in the very early days of your career registering as self-employed might make more sense. In some countries you are allowed to pay yourself in dividends (which has its own benefits) when registered as a company, but the tax you pay may also be higher as a result.

REGISTERING FOR VAT (VALUE ADDED TAX)

You only really need to worry about registering for VAT once you make over a certain amount of revenue in most countries. VAT is a tax that may need to be added to the sale price of artworks once you are registered. It will be payable in certain countries and not others, and has shipping and insurance implications too. Registering for VAT lets you reclaim this tax on some purchases, but might not be a concern until later in your career.

EXPENSES

As an artist, there will be a fair amount of flexibility with what you can claim as an expense. Art materials and studio rent are a given. If you buy tickets to a museum or theatre production, a case can be made for these being research trips. If you go out for dinner with a curator, this makes sense as an expense too. If you buy new clothes for an opening and you can prove their necessity, this may also be justifiable. Usually, your expenses are deducted from the total amount earned, and your tax is calculated on the remainder.

TAX-FREE ALLOWANCE

In most countries there is a certain threshold below which you won't have to pay any tax at all. How much you pay after that will depend on your earnings – once you exceed the threshold, the percentage rate you pay increases only on earnings *above* it, not on those below.

WORKING AND FILING A SEPARATE TAX RETURN

Many artists have jobs on the side, and so will need to file a tax return as well as being taxed by the company they work for. This tax is calculated separately, all you need to do is indicate how much you earned and how much tax you paid through your other job on your tax return.

KEEP YOUR RECEIPTS

If you are going to file anything as an expense you have to prove that you did indeed pay for it, and must also be able to justify it as a legitimate expense necessary for your business. Keeping your receipts is the simplest way of doing this, but it also means you must add these up manually and keep a record. Nowadays there are many apps and software platforms that can do all of this for you if you photograph or scan your receipts, though some require monthly subscriptions.

INVOICING

Invoices will most likely become a necessary part of the admin you will have to complete regularly. There are many free invoice templates online, and as long as it includes the key details, the actual layout doesn't really matter. (See 'Making an Invoice', p. 192, for more details.)

KEEPING TRACK

The best way to keep track of all of your accounts is to use a spreadsheet. Any payment received should be recorded on one tab, and any expense on a separate one. Include as many details as you can, so that you can prove everything in the unlikely event you are audited by your tax authority. There are many apps and services available that will keep track of all expenses and payments, including sending out invoices for you, but again these will often charge a monthly subscription.

HIRING AN ACCOUNTANT

There are many arts-specialist accountants out there, often affordable and experienced in all the topics you may have questions about. It is possible to file your tax return yourself, but this will require a little research on your part.

FILING EARLY, NOT ON TIME

Each country will have differing dates for this, but to use the UK as an example: if you are self-employed, the tax year ends in April. You then have until the end of the following January to file your return and pay your tax. Many artists seem to wait until the January deadline to file their tax return and then must pay the tax owed in one big lump sum, as well as a penalty for any late payment. If you file your return as early as possible you will have a much longer interval to pay off the tax due, in incremental payments if necessary. This is a lot less stressful, and a bit of pre-planning makes your life far easier in the long run.

Filing your taxes is something that may seem daunting because of its complexity and the legal implications. These factors can lead artists to put off registering for tax, postpone filing their tax return, or avoid it altogether. The more successful you become the more unavoidable accounting will be, and so it is advisable to take the time to learn about what it means and how it is done as early as possible.

Making an Invoice

Once you start selling work, you are going to need to issue invoices. It's an incredibly simple (and useful) document that you will use now and for the rest of your career. If you create a good template, you can add the details specific to each sale while leaving the rest of it as is.

The importance of a professional invoice shouldn't be understated. If someone is paying you their hard-earned money for something you've created, the way you invoice them could make them begin to question their decision if it isn't done correctly. In all dealings with potential buyers, you want to give an air of professionalism and dependability, and a poorly formatted invoice (or no invoice at all) is a surefire way to undermine that. There are legal ramifications too: if you are ever in the unfortunate position of having to pursue someone legally for non-payment of funds, having sent a good-quality invoice at the start will make your case much stronger.

Most word-processing software will have a good invoice template already saved, but you can also download one from the internet.

Below is a list of everything that needs to be included on an invoice, with a short explanation for each.

YOUR NAME Your full name, as well as any pseudonym or artist name. If you are a limited company or similar you will need the registered company name on here too.

YOUR ADDRESS The registered business address. If you don't have one, use your home address.

YOUR CONTACT DETAILS Email and phone number are the bare minimum, but there's no reason not to put your website address here too.

DATE This is the date you sent the invoice, not the date the sale was agreed, or the date the work was delivered.

INVOICE NUMBER This is to help you identify which invoice is which – you should be keeping track of these in a separate document. It's advisable to have a spreadsheet in which you input all of your sales, and (on a separate tab) all your expenses. This will help when it comes to finalizing your accounts, so include the invoice number next to every sale on here too. A good format for these would be something like 252601: the 25 and 26 correspond to the 2025/2026 tax year; 01 is the number of invoices issued that year so far, and so would increase by one with each invoice. For example, the second would read 252602, and so on.

BUYER'S NAME Their full name, as well as the name of the company if applicable.

BUYER'S ADDRESS This is important as it helps to identify the buyer further.

BUYER'S CONTACT DETAILS Email and phone number are sufficient here.

DESCRIPTION OF THE SALE ITEM What it is they are buying. Title, dimensions, materials and a short description will be sufficient here, but some artists also choose to include a thumbnail photograph.

QUANTITY How many of this item the buyer is purchasing. If they are buying multiple separate works it is always a good idea to include them as separate items to avoid any potential confusion.

PRICE This should be the price you have already agreed with the buyer – there should be no surprises here.

SUBTOTAL This should be in the currency the buyer will be paying in, which should have been agreed ahead of time. If you quote the price in one currency and the buyer pays in another, the exchange rate at the time of payment will likely be different to what it was when you sent the invoice, and the totals won't match.

DEDUCTIONS This is where you can deduct any gallery percentages (if invoicing a gallery), any discounts as agreed, or any production costs if applicable. It's a good idea to have these recorded rather than just deducted from the final total as it could be necessary to prove the total price, the discount amount, and that the discount has already been deducted.

VAT OR TAX APPLIED Depending on the specifics of the sale and your career, you may legally be required to charge tax on a sale. This differs based upon where you and the buyer are located, so it's essential to work out the responsibilities of each party before completing the invoice.

TOTAL How much the invoice is for. This will be the amount that the buyer is required to pay you after any deductions.

YOUR BANK DETAILS Including the requisite details for both domestic and international transfers.

YOUR VAT OR TAX NUMBER If you have one.

YOUR PAYMENT TERMS The date by which you expect payment. This should be agreed ahead of time with the buyer. There are legal limits on how long people are able to delay paying an invoice, which vary depending on where in the world both parties are, but these can be extended or shortened if agreed by both parties. If you decide on an arbitrary amount of time and include this on your invoice without having agreed it with the buyer beforehand (and in writing), they are well within their rights to delay payment until the end of the *legal* window of time, regardless of how long your invoice states, so don't aggressively chase up your payments until they are outside that legal window.

THANK YOU All business transactions from the very beginning to the very end should be as courteous and as professional as possible.

THE LEGAL RIGHTS OF BOTH PARTIES This is something you may or may not choose to include. If you do, don't make it too aggressive. This can generally be set in fairly small text, and should specify the law governing payment terms in whichever country or economic area is relevant.

A final note: always ensure that your invoice is sent on time, to the correct address, and that all the information on it is correct. It is also a good idea to save it as a PDF, as some mobile and computer operating systems won't be able to open certain files whereas a PDF is universal.

What Does Success Look Like?

For most artists, the need to keep making art is the driving force of their practice. Artmaking begins as a pastime, becomes a passion and eventually (if you're lucky) also turns into a career.

The transition from pastime to passion is a gradual one, perhaps occurring unnoticed, until it is the motivation that gets you up in the morning and fills your day with excitement. At this stage, you might spend hours dreaming about making art as a career and the freedom that this will bring. Nothing sounds more ideal than your hobby becoming your job, but once this is achieved, the stresses that it will bring can dull the joy you once found in it. Deadlines pile on the pressure, and having to sell works to pay the bills can limit the freedom to experiment that you enjoyed when money wasn't an issue.

Success means different things to different people. If you measure your success by money, fame and respect, you will always be looking not at what you have achieved, but at whatever the next step of progression is. You will not be appreciating your past achievements but looking towards future (as yet unachieved) goals. At one point in your career, success would have felt like selling your first painting, but each success repositions your view of the next one. With every achievement you are left yearning.

Success should be measured instead by your ability to retain the joy in making. For many artists that joy diminishes once the stresses of success begin to make them forget why they began making art in the first place. Whatever stage of your career you are at, if you haven't let the stresses intrinsic to being an artist weigh you down and you can still make works with joy, you are succeeding. Remember why you started making art in the first place, and continue to remind yourself of what your dreams and aspirations were at the beginning of your artistic career, as it's likely that you have achieved many of them already. Try not to forget what successes you have had and, when you do think of the future, focus on what exciting things are yet to come. If you are able to do this, you are moving in the right direction.

Conclusion

Being an artist is hard. It's challenging recreationally, and even harder as a career. Not only are the skills difficult to master, but it takes a strong resolution and unshakeable self-belief to even be pursued. There can be no definitive guides for how success in this career is to be pursued, and so we hope that with this guide we have gone some way not towards telling you how to do this, but towards helping you find the tools with which to forge your own path. We can't do this for you, and nor would we assume to be able to, because as an artist you are naturally unique, resilient and fiercely creative. Your career will be uniquely yours, and whatever highs and lows this journey will necessarily involve, they will all contribute to forming the work that is born out of the struggle. By reading this book, if nothing else, you have shown yourself to be resolute in the pursuit of that goal, and that alone is immensely commendable.

Let our closing words be this: work hard, try not to compare yourself to others, worry less, and try to retain the joy in artmaking through it all. If you are able to achieve those things, you have already succeeded.

Further Reading

As we have said multiple times, and will never cease saying, there is no one way to succeed. All artists' careers are different, and there is no one-size-fits-all recipe for success. That being said, it would be impossible to write this kind of book without acknowledging the wealth of information out there that can help you in your goal.

We would recommend devouring as much advice about the business side of art as you can find. Read up on marketing, sales, tax, branding, accounting and social media. Some of it will be relevant and some of it won't, but you'll probably find a few nuggets of wisdom in even the weakest of sources.

Below are some books we have read and can vouch for – the authors know what they are talking about, and these six recommendations would be a good starting line-up for your continued journey of self-education.

David Bayles and Ted Orland, *Art & Fear: Observations on the Perils (and Rewards) of Artmaking* (1993)
This book is so great that we read it in a single sitting.

Heather Darcy Bhandari and Jonathan Melber, *Art/work: Everything You Need to Know (and Do) As You Pursue Your Art Career* (2009)
This should be everyone's go-to book for all things art career related. It should be required reading for all arts courses.

Rosalind Davis and Annabel Tilley, *What They Didn't Teach You in Art School* (2016)
Rosalind was a contributor to our first book, and hers is still one of the staples of the genre. Highly recommended.

Adrian George, *The Curator's Handbook: Museums, Commercial Galleries, Independent Spaces* (2024)
All artists should have at least a basic understanding of what curation involves – not just because curating oneself can be useful for your career on the whole, but also because understanding what galleries are doing on your behalf can aid in those relationships.

Will Gompertz, *What Are You Looking At?: The Surprising, Shocking, and Sometimes Strange Story of 150 Years of Modern Art* (2012)
This book is an excellent distillation of the history of art, from the Impressionists until (almost) the present day. As well as being a highly enjoyable read, it is always important for artists to have an understanding of the environment in which they work theoretically, contextually and historically.

Gilda Williams, *How to Write About Contemporary Art* (2014)
Writing about art, both yours and other people's, is likely to become more important to your career than you may anticipate. This book does an excellent job at laying bare exactly how to do so.

Here are some other books on the same subject that come highly recommended:

- Frances Ambler, *Brief Lessons in Creativity* (2019)
- Michael Atavar, *How to Be an Artist* (2009)
- Holly Black, *Artists on Art: How They See, Think & Create* (2022)
- James Cahill, *Ways of Being: Advice for Artists by Artists* (2018)
- Michael Craig-Martin, *On Being An Artist* (2015)
- Will Gompertz, *Think Like an Artist ... and Lead a More Creative, Productive Life* (2016)
- Austin Kleon, *Keep Going: 10 Ways to Stay Creative in Good Times and Bad* (2019)
- Marion Milner, *On Not Being Able to Paint* (2010)
- Kent Nerburn, *The Artist's Journey: On Making Art & Being an Artist* (2020)
- Grayson Perry, *Playing to the Gallery: Helping Contemporary Art in Its Struggle to Be Understood* (2014)
- Magnus Resch, *How to Become a Successful Artist* (2021)
- Rainer Maria Rilke, *Letters to a Young Painter* (1920-6; republished 2017)
- Rick Rubin, *The Creative Act: A Way of Being* (2023)
- Jerry Saltz, *How to Be an Artist* (2020)
- Bob and Roberta Smith, *You Are an Artist* (2020)
- Kit White, *101 Things to Learn in Art School* (2011)

About the Authors

Benjamin Murphy is an artist and writer. Originally from West Yorkshire, he now lives with his wife Oona in Helsinki, Finland. His primary focus is in making large-scale charcoal on raw canvas artworks, which he exhibits in galleries globally. Since his first exhibition in 2012 his work has been included in more than 200 exhibitions, and he has had multiple solo shows. Alongside being an artist and writer, Murphy lectures at arts universities worldwide, and has a bachelor's degree and two master's degrees in the arts. He also enjoys reading, boxing, skateboarding and befriending animals.
benjaminmurphy.info

Nick JS Thompson is an artist and curator originally from Oxfordshire but has lived and worked in London for over a decade. He held positions as a gallery manager at a commercial gallery before co-founding Delphian Gallery. He has curated almost 70 exhibitions and exhibited his own work in the UK and internationally. He now lives in southwest France with his wife Jen and dog, Betty.
nickjsthompson.format.com

About the Contributors

Paul Foster is Director of the Saatchi Gallery, London.

Lori Fitzgerald is a director of psychotherapy and mentoring with over twenty-five years' experience in supporting artists and creatives with their mental health.

Wingshan is an artist and curator based in Nottingham, UK.

Dr Charley Peters is a practising artist and is Head of Graduate School at City & Guilds of London Art School.

Index

First published in the United Kingdom in 2026 by
Thames & Hudson Ltd, 6–24 Britannia Street, London WC1X 9JD

First published in the United States of America in 2026 by
Thames & Hudson Inc., 500 Fifth Avenue, New York, New York 10110

The Artist's Roadmap: Practical Strategies for a Career in Art

EU Authorized Representative: Interart S.A.R.L.
19 rue Charles Auray, 93500 Pantin, Paris, France
productsafety@thameshudson.co.uk
interart.fr

A CIP catalogue record for this book is available from the British Library

Library of Congress Control Number 2024950049

ISBN 978-0-500-29839-8
01

Printed in China by Shenzhen Reliance Printing Co. Ltd

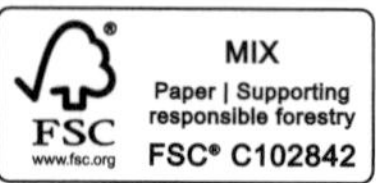

Be the first to know about our new releases,
exclusive content and author events by visiting
thamesandhudson.com
thamesandhudsonusa.com
thamesandhudson.com.au